Hope Unborn, Unborn, Unborn

By

John G. Carswell

1stBooks - rev. 01/19/02

<u>DEDICATION</u>

This book is dedicated to my wife, Rubye. She has been by my side, supported me, and has given me advise all the way.

To my wife Rubye who has taught me about family, love, happiness, and made me have confidence within myself.

We were married in 1963, and we still share the greatest times together. She is the love of my life, and my best friend. We always make each other happy.

To my children Martin (Marty), and Reo whom I love tremendously, and try to give support. I always value time spent with them, whether it was to nurture, play, teach, or share with them.

To them a rich history on Carswells, Jenkins, Irvins, Martins, Smiths, and Hightowers that they will be proud to have, for a family heritage and keep "Hope Unborn, Unborn" alive to be reborn in the proper places in them.

1999—
—John G. Carswell

TABLE OF CONTENTS

<u>INTRODUCTION</u>

The founding fathers of the "status quo" major league baseball teams (USA) did not set out to create a major league based on equality; otherwise the need for this book would not be necessary…at least part of it would not. It would have been stated in the by-laws of professional baseball initially if they had well intentions.

When the United Stated of America was founded, it was very much formed in a similar way…"equal rights," slave labor, and justice for some.

My hope is that this book will be educational, particularly to our youth. My dream is that the struggle against racism will be helped, and hopefully it will help ease the pain of omission, and help bond our history and culture so that it will be realized anew.

The realization is that history cannot be done over on this matter, but an attempt can be made to make it right.

Recognition and acceptance by the total community of baseball in American will go along ways to satisfy that correction. The total community of baseball has been in denial about the *real* truth since the first time contracts were denied, and teams refused to play because of the color of another player, which was in the mid-1880's.

From the time Frank Duncan was denied a contract, or George Stovey wasn't allowed to pitch, or Fleetwood Walker wasn't allowed to catch, and Cap Anson had the power to stop his team from playing because he did not want to lower himself to be caught on the baseball field with a Black man something has been wrong with baseball.

I have partly been inspired to write this book by Branch Rickey's statement when he said, *"Human kind and all men, anthropological, come from the same source, with the same potentials, must have a potential equality in <u>chance and opportunity.</u>"*

What particularly caught my ear was "chance and opportunity." When considering any of the persons I feel worthy of Hall Of Fame recognition, these were the words that best fit in all of the categories (mentioned in Chapter VI) necessary to make this a fair assessment to the people responsible for the growth, development, and maintenance of the Negro Leagues.

It was particularly interesting to me that the Negro League players had the "chance and opportunity" to serve in World Wars I & II, but were denied the opportunity to have freedoms in the same country that they served well and died for.

Although conditions were restricted in both World Wars in the form of separate but equal, they were still in the service.

In baseball, the <u>major leagues</u> were divided into the Negro Leagues and the "status quo leagues." My Uncle Thomas Hightower wrote a book about the conditions of the Black soldier in World War I, and we saw the same conditions reoccur in the Jackie Robinson story.

African-Americans were not allowed to participate organizationally in the "status quo" league even under the same conditions that were afforded in the service. Despite these obstacles, I found that many Negro League players were college men, and of course, they had to attend Black colleges.

All Negro Major League player's records should be submitted into THE record books. The Negro League experience is not only African-American history, it is American history.

When Fleetwood Walker, the first African-American major leaguer, and the rest of the Black players begin making their presence known, the "status quo" realized that they were just a few years from slavery, and they did not deserve to be treated as "regular" human beings, or fellow citizens…at least not regular baseball players.

Apparently, if they wanted to play baseball, they needed to play with their own, and for their own, and be accepted and recognized by their own.

Well, I'm here to recognize them, and set the records straight for the rights of a people denied "chance and opportunity" in their own country, in a land they fought and died for. So racism and all its rudiments had its beginnings in the 1880's for professional baseball.

"Hope Unborn, Unborn" is an attempt to show how from the conception of professional baseball in America to the present, deserving and brave Americans, particularly African-Americans have weathered a storm, and need to be equally recognized as their counterparts are.

We will see how the sports world has changed, and how professional baseball and amateur sports need to recognized their problems, and make an honest attempt to change.

The lack of exposure on a cross the board major league level in America, at that time created a domino effect in the Black community in high schools, colleges, etc. Even businesses and the job market, and the *real* reason why the SAT, ACT, and other standards have been used.

The result of that microcosm is what created in baseball, the Negro Leagues. The result of that microcosm in education, is what created the testing systems, Black colleges and universities. The result of that microcosm in the job market is what created model cities programs and similar type programs in the Black community that failed.

Former Negro League players struggled (over 100 years), and are still struggling along with their children and families, because of the way they have been treated, or the lack there of.

The Polish-Americans, the Jewish-Americans, and Hispanic-Americans all represent people who have struggled in America. However, no American ethnic group has experienced racism and problems of assimilation in America in general, and baseball in particular as the African-American has simply because of their skin color.

I contend that in the early transition of baseball (late 40's & early 50's), when the Negro League players were being assimilated in the current major leagues, in most cases the _real stars_ of the Negro Leagues didn't need to be sent to the minor leagues for an "adjustment period." I believe the major leagues did this to create a sense of superiority, and of course for prejudicial reasons.

Larry Doby was the second player taken shortly after Jackie Robinson, and he didn't need an "adjustment period". Why would greater stars than either of the two of them at that time need adjusting?

Doby was one of the few cases where he was allowed to go directly to the apparent baseball club that signed him. Most Negro League stars signed by the major leagues were sent directly to the minors, which made them feel inadequate.

If they knew they were of major league caliber, then why would players like Jackie Robinson, Roy Campanella, and Monte Irvin, need an "adjustment period?" Ernie Banks didn't need an adjustment period, and look what happen to him?

Ray Dandridge, a hall of famer, was just 35 when he was signed by the New York Giants in 1949, but they elected to let him spend his "adjustment period" buried in the minor leagues.

During those last three years he hit. 363, .311, and .324. Not only did Ray Dandrige lose because of "chance and opportunity", but the Giants lost a valuable opportunity to help themselves and the whole baseball community. If Ray had Hall of Fame credentials, and he did, why sign him and send him to the minor leagues? Could it be to embarrass the Negro League stars? Maybe.

After the Brooklyn Dodgers signed Jackie in 1945, he went to Venezuela in the winter to play on a Black all-star team. After expressing doubt about prospective abilities in the "status quo" major leagues to his roommate Gene Benson, he was convinced by Benson that the pitching in the Negro Leagues was just as good as the pitching in the "status quo" league. Robinson and others spent time in the minor leagues that they didn't need to experience.

Negro League stars trying to prove their worth to the clubs that signed them wasted valuable time. They had no choice regardless of their super star status in the Negro Leagues.

What was suppose to happen to a player coming from the Negro Major Leagues to the "status quo league" to make him need an "adjustment period?"

I don't recall reading anything about an "adjustment period" for Black soldiers in World Wars I & II when they gave their all. I wonder why?

Roy Campanella is a prime example of what I mean. He spent 9 years in the Negro Leagues with a batting average of. 353. He had a. 364 all-star batting average. When the Brooklyn Dodgers signed him, he was a proven top veteran player of the Negro Leagues. The Dodgers sent Roy to the minor leagues for over 2 years. There he had combined B. A. of. 296, and won the MVP award the two seasons he was there.

To say that one proven Negro League star veteran was not ready for the "status quo" major leagues is to say that none was ready, because there was no legitimate reason. Again, all Negro Major League star's records should be a part of all major league records, and all Negro major league records a part of the major league records.

In "HOPE UNBORN, UNBORN", I hope to show where Negro League players, and support people, (owners, managers, and founders) have a right, and should be recognized, and someone needs to be responsible to make it happen. I will show where the Hall of Fame voting has to be changed whether it's writers and/or a committee.

I started working on this book in 1994, and some Negro League players I've supported for the HOF have been recently selected (Willie Wells, Bullet Joe Rogan, Cool Papa Bell, Larry Doby, and Smokey Joe Williams), but many more deserving NL veterans have not been. There are also many non-Negro League players that I have supported are not in the HOF. Players such as Orlando Cepeda, Pete Rose, Tony Oliva, Gil Hodges, Al Oliver, Maury Wills, Bruce Sutter and more at this writing.

The Brooklyn Dodgers, and the Detroit Tigers (despite the problems they created) helped me to grow up and understand baseball in America.

Players like Willie Mays, Hank Aaron, Ernie Banks, Roberto Clemente, Minnie Minoso, and Larry Doby were all non-Dodger favorites of mind.

A salute, a big salute to the "boys of summer," who made contributions to my childhood, and also my manhood.

*   Smokey Joe Williams, Orlando Cepeda and Larry Doby were recently selected to the HOF-1999.

*   Norman Turkey was added in 2000.

Ode to the Negro Leagues

Sad to say it was the color of your skin,
You were good citizens, but you were just not let in.
Our heroes in good times, our heroes in bad,
In the early years, you never, never had—a chance.
On the road to reach a heroes' goal,
You were our hope unborn, untried, and our story untold.
Nobly you waited. With dignity you sought to actualize your true potentials.
*   You were our role models, but others were without interest in your credentials.*
Courageously, you traveled to far away lands.
*   For opportunity to take a stand, and then be accepted as a man—with a dream.*
In Mexico, Cuba, and other places you toiled.
While honing your skills on distant soil.
No longer to struggle with respect and rejection,
Other countries welcomed you, and you received real affection.
Though these were temporary places for off-season,
'T was a time of obscurity, and not a good reason.
For what were the hopes of Paige, Gibson, and Wells?
Your stories are legendary, and we are the ones who will tell—the truth.
We've too heard about the hopes of Irvin, Lloyd, and Day,
Barnstorming talents of Black baseball on display.
We'll not let them forget.
We should teach them our own history.
We must not allow it to remain a dark mystery.
*   Let it be solved here in baseball,*
*   Let it be solved forever and for all.*

—John G. Carswell
Rubye A. Carswell
1994

CHAPTER I: MY DODGER BLUES WERE BLACK

The late forties and fifties were the times that I grew up in. This was a time when the world was supposedly at peace. A time when the country was beginning to rebuild and recover from the war. A time before "under God" was written into our flag pledge. A time when people would close the doors to their houses, but not necessarily lock them. A time when my grandfather, the Rev. Dr. George John Martin owned the only television set in our neighborhood. It was a time when African-Americans gathered around the television set when word spread that a Black person was scheduled to be on. A time when the Yankees and the Dodgers were the only "real baseball teams," at least the only ones that seemed to matter. A time to remember, and a time to forget…wow! what a time of history.

This was a time for our country to heal, but unfortunately, it was also a time to bleed. Too much of the good of that past has been forgotten, and too much of the bad has been remembered. However, all of our history needs to make us aware of our present, and our future.

Educationally, we have placed most of our interest in mathematics and English…and rightly so. Nevertheless, I'm not so sure that history, because of what it teaches us about the past is not the most valuable subject matter.

It has been said that sports is a reflective microcosm of our society. Well, I do know that our society has a way of being forgiving, and also a way of being unforgiving at the same time, and such is sports.

I grew up in a town in the south, Lakeland, Florida (central Florida), "the world's citrus center." Lakeland is the spring training home of the Detroit Tigers. As was most cities in the south during that time, it was racially divided to the same extent as sports was, both professionally and amateur.

A few teams (Cubs, Giants, Indians, and possibly another team) trained in Arizona, but most of them, 16 at the time, trained in Florida. The Florida teams (called the Grapefruit League) would come every spring to play the Tigers, as they still do every spring.

Although the Detroit Tigers played in my hometown, they were not the team that I learned to love, and neither did the Black community. The reason we did not identify with the Tigers was because they didn't have any African-American players on the team at that time, but they could have. I know this from first hand experience.

My Uncle Melzie Pressley, and my father-in-law, Gilbert Jenkins spoke often of Jimmy (Squab) Hill a diminutive little left-handed pitcher from my hometown.

They said that Squab was a major league caliber pitcher. Those baseball savvy guys felt that he certainly belonged in the "status quo" major leagues, because he was of major league stock.

Squab often pitched batting practice for the Detroit Tigers in spring training, and HOFer Hank Greenberg and his teammates who claimed that Squab was definitely a major league pitcher attested his abilities. Fortunately, for Squab, he had a 13-year productive career (1938-50) in the Negro Leagues. His best years were with the Newark Eagles (1938-45).

The highlights of his career, which also tells of his abilities in 1941, when he pitched hitless relief in an East-West All Star mid-season game, and he beat Satchel Paige in a North-South All Star game at the end of the same season.

When the Brooklyn Dodgers came to play the Detroit Tigers at Henley Field, they brought with them my **Black Dodgers Blue** heroes. The original group I loved was Jackie, Roy Campanella, and Don Newcombe. Sandy Amoros, Joe Black, Chico Fernandez, and Junior Gilliam later joined them.

Then there were the Yankees with their pin stripes. Big stars like Mickey Mantle, Yogi Berra, Whitey Ford, Bill Skrown, Elston Howard, and others. Strange thing, I always hated the Yankees even after they had Elston Howard, an African-American.

Other teams had their first great Black stars. The Cleveland Indians had Larry Doby, the Milwaukee Braves had the great Hank Aaron, the New York Giants had the talented Willie Mays, and Monte Irvin, the Pittsburgh Pirates had Roberto Clemente, and finally the Chicago White Sox had the versatile Minnie Minoso after he had a cup of java with Cleveland.

I'd love to see these other players and teams as they came to play the Tigers. As much as I didn't like the Yankees, I hated the Tigers more. I failed to see how a town with a great African-American population did not have a Black representative on the team, or in their organization.

When national television made its grand broadcasting entry into the city of quaint provincial land of the many lakes, I heard mostly Dizzy Dean and his partner, Buddy Blatter, "brought to you by Falstaff beer," and some cigarette as the broadcast went!

Dizzy and Buddy would recount days of yesteryear about the greatness of the 1927 Yankees, the 1934 Cardinals, or one of the "status quo" major league teams. They would tout tales about the greatness of Gehrig, Ruth, Jackson (shoeless), Stan "the man" Musial, the Gas House Gang, and the Whiz Kids. Unfortunate for me, because the only one of that group that I could relate to was Stan Musial. Stan was still playing in my era.

In addition, those great players didn't get the chance to prove how really great they were, because certain groups of people were excluded, namely African-Americans, and dark skin Hispanics. Oh I know Dizzy talked about how he faced Satchel Paige and the Pittsburgh Crawfords, the St Louis Stars, and the Homestead Grays in games from time to time. But that was in exhibition/barnstorming games...entertainment as it were, and not for the official record books.

I am aware of this every time I here records today being discussed, or compared to the ones in the sacred past. The NML players get little or no recognition even though they were organized (1920).

By identifying with my Black Dodgers Blues, I later learn to identify with all the Dodger Blues. I became a Duke Snider, Gil Hodges, Carl Furillo, Clem Labine, and an all Dodger fan of the Dodger Blue.

So here I was a Black child, living in a southern town, (Lakeland, Florida), where the Detroit Tigers trained, and a fan of the Brooklyn Dodgers, who trained in Vero Beach, Florida, and played in Brooklyn, New York.

I was disappointed that I could only see the Dodgers in person only once or twice a year. One year, Jackie Robinson didn't come. They claimed he either playing in a B game, or he was injured. Either way, I didn't believe it, and I was really brokenhearted.

In basketball, I was also a big fan of the Boston Celtics. This was mostly because of my interest in Bill Russell, K. C. Jones, Sam Jones, and Satch Sanders. Later, I learned to admire the whole team. Particularly Bob Cousy, Bill Sherman, Frank Ramsey, and of course John Havilacek. It was a growing process for me.

In recent years my friend, now deceased, Cecil Clark use to get on me about being a fan of the Boston Celtics, because he called Boston a racist town. My point to him was, I loved the team because there were players on the team that I identified with, not the town of Boston.

When the Brooklyn Dodgers came to Lakeland to play the Tigers, I identified with the players, not Brooklyn, New York. In fact, until 1955, (when the Dodgers became champs), I had never been to Brooklyn, New York. My problem with Cecil was that he was a Yankee fan, and I could not stand the Yankees.

What excited me about the Dodgers Blues was the way I thought they handled themselves, and to see African-Americans play at that level as other players did.

I use to see Jackie Robinson get on base, and the pitcher would just come unglued. I saw this happen to great pitchers. I have seen at this point, Maury Wills, Lou Brock, Otis Nixon and Rickey Henderson all in their prime. These are not just four of the best base stealers of my time, but of all time.

Jackie didn't steal as many bases as these fellows, but he put more excitement and personality into the art of base stealing. Jackie seemed as though he knew the pitcher personally, and what it took to get him upset. Of course, Jackie like Maury Wills was already 28 years old as a Dodger rookie, and spent time in the Negro Leagues and the military.

///

"MY FAVORITES AND WHY"

Now I would like to take a walk through my Dodger Blues to *name my* all-time Dodger favorites at each position, and tell why.

Starting with number two on your scorecard, the catcher for me has to be *Roy Campanella.* If Campanella had had a long "accepted" major league career, I don't think a catcher that I have ever seen could come close to him in most areas. My first comparison was Mike Piazza, a great catcher, but lacks the defense and great arm Campy had. My next thought was Charley Johnson, but he lacks the bat power, and pitcher support. Johnny Bench is the closest to what I think Campanella was. Roy was a complete catcher. He personified catching, if you will. His build, his demeanor, his readiness, his fielding, batting, defense, and great arm represented all of the things you would want in a catcher.

I've heard and read about Miz Mackey, (Campy's mentor) Josh Gibson, and Mickey Cochrane, even Bruce Petway, but I did not see any of those great players. The only catcher in Campanella's time to compare...him with was Yogi Berra. In my assessment, Campanella was quicker, had a more accurate arm, and also had more power.

Unfortunately, his career was shorten because of an accident, and the fact that he couldn't play earlier because of the "color line." Another reason to add his NL records.

Number three on the scorecard would be the first baseman. My all-time Dodger Blue first baseman is *Gil Hodges.* Gil had what I called the Dodger Blue charisma. One time in Lakeland against the Tigers, I saw Gil Hodges make a play that I've never seen before or since. There was a ground ball to shortstop on a very fast runner. The throw from the shortstop to first was very high. It was so high until Gil had to leap as high as he could to glove the ball. While he was hanging in air, he made a scissors type move with his legs causing his back foot to hit the base on his downward flight, a split second before the runner got to first base. What a play, what a player?...should be in the HOF.

On your scorecard for number four is the all-time second baseman. Although he was not one of my orginal Dodger Blues, *Junior Gilliam* is my all-time Dodger Blue second baseman. He was a good fielder, a switch hitter, and a quiet leader, with great bat control. Junior rarely struck out, and could lead off or bat second.

Going to number six on the scorecard is the shortstop. That would be HOFer, *Pee Wee Reese.* Pee Wee has to be the all-time Dodger Blue shortstop.

The youngsters today know him mostly because of his association, and initiation of the Pee Wee Reese Little League around the country. He was the one for me to take charge of that ball coming from the shortstop position. The HOFer was also a great clutch hitter. He was also the captain of the team.

He did not have an entire career at the position, but HOFer ***Jackie Robinson*** is on my scorecard for the number five position as the all-time third baseman. I might have been encouraged by the number of times I saw the man from the "hot corner" steal home base. Of course, Jackie played other positions, but from what I saw, third base appeared to be his best spot.

He is not a Hall of Famer, but the hall of fame play he made helped convince me that he was worthy. My all-time Dodger Blue left fielder is ***Sandy Amoros.*** I'm sure he was not the best hitting left fielder in Dodger Blue history, but he is the one I want to see go and get that ball out of the stands. He did this in the 1955 series off of Yogi Berra's bat. That was his moment in time for me. His bat didn't have a potent display of power like Campanella, Snider, or Hodges, but we loved to see him wag that bat back and forth as he waited on just the right pitch. However, Sandy did have surprising power.

This HOF center fielder was compared to Willie Mays and Mickey Mantle all the time during my childhood. My all-time Dodger Blue man in center field is "the Duke", ***Duke Snider.*** He was called up a few days after Jackie Robinson arrived in 1947. Willie Davis was faster, and his speed helped him to be a better base stealer, but Duke had speed, power, and was a timely hitter. As an outfielder, he was very graceful. Duke was what I called Mr. Excitement. He had one the hardest swings that I have ever seen. I compare his power to that of Mantle, Jackson, Easter, Sosa, and McGwire. Suitcase Simpson swung as hard, but not as effectively as Duke did.

Duke hit a ball at Henley Field (Lakeland), that I believed they never found…must have been close to 600 feet easily.

There has only been four players in my life time that I would compare this right fielder's arm to. Roberto Clemente, George (Shotgun) Shula, Raul Mondesi, and Rocky Colavito. That all-time Dodger Blue right fielder is ***Carl Furillo.*** Once while I was visiting relatives in New York City, we attended a game in Brooklyn. It was a game against the Cincinnati Reds (Redlegs at that time). I saw Carl Furillo field a ball about 20 feet from the warning track, slip down, and still throw out a runner from his knees at home plate. What an arm the "Redding Riffle" had. He was also a good hitter with very good power.

When I played baseball, I was a pitcher, basically. I've been watching, playing, or coaching baseball since 1948. The greatest pitcher my eyes have seen was ***Sandy Koufax,*** bar none. In the beginning of his fabulous career when Sandy was a "bonus baby," he had a rough time. It seemed like every outing was an adventure. He could not be sent down to the farm club because of the "bonus baby" rule. That rule says that a player had to remain on the major league team roster for at least two years.

Sandy Koufax righted himself and became the complete HOF pitcher that we all saw. With a sound arm, he probably could have easily won over 400 games.

The Dodgers had one other lefty with the potential of Koufax. That guy was Carl Spooner, but he developed arm problems early in his career. Sandy is the all-time Dodger Blue left handed pitcher.

As hard as I tried, I could not decide on one right hander for the all-time Dodger Blue team…so there are two HOF greats, instead of one. **Don Drysdale, Don Sutton and Don Newcombe**, Big D, Little D, and Big Newk. Two of power, and the other of finesse. Big D (Drysdale) was just overpowering with a whip like three-quarter-arm motion. Little D (Sutton) pitched the way you would want to teach your son how to pitch. Newk was just power. We loved to see him pitch and over match hitters in the Dodger Blue uniform. I hated to see him face Hank Aaron though, I wonder why?

Drysdale would hit streaks were he was just unhittable for innings. In fact, he held the record for the most consecutive shutout innings pitched, 58. It has since been broken at this writing by another former Dodger great, Orel Hershiser at 59 innings. Sutton, Drysdale, and Big Newk are the co-all time Dodger Blue right handed pitchers.

This guy was not an original Dodger Blue, but **Manny Mota** is the Dodger Blue all-time pinch-hitter. Manny is just simply the best Dodger Blue pinch-hitter I've seen. His timely hits were the greatest.

In the beginning of his career, he was a starter. Walter Alston, the then Dodger manager changed him to one of the greatest relievers of his time. The only other reliever at that time to compare him to was Elroy Face. The all-time Dodger Blue right handed reliever is **Clem Labine.** Clem was before the concept of saves. It is hard to know accurately how many saves he had, because the concept is a relatively new one at the time.

Ron Perronoski is the all-time left-handed closer. He was a very dependable reliever. During a time when managers were beginning to pitch lefty against lefty, and right hander against right hander, Perronoski was as equally successful with right handers.

This is the all-time Dodger Blue baseball team (time considered 1948-1970).

> *Ist Base—Gil Hodges*
> *2nd Base—Junior Gilliam*
> *3rd Base—Jackie Robinson*
> *Shortstop—Pee Wee Reese*
> *Catcher—Roy Campanella*
> *Left Fielder—Sandy Amoros*
> *Center Fielder—Duke Snider*
> *Right Fielder—Carl Furillo*
> *Left Handed Pitcher—Sandy Koufax*

*** Right Handed Pitchers—Don Drysdale,**
Don Sutton
Pinch Hitter—Manny Mota
*** Manager—Walter Alston,**
***Announcers—Red Barber,**
Vin Scully
Left Handed Reliever—Ron Perronoski
Right Handed Reliever—Clem Labine
* Indicates two people at the same position.

These players, managers, and announcers argumentatively may, or may not be the best at their respective positions in the Dodger Blue era specified, but these are my Dodger Blues, and that's the way I remembered the Dodger Blue teams.

ROLE MODELS

One of the positions today I take exception to is that *"athletes are role models."* I know none of these people personally. Therefore, I cannot say that they were role models for me. I admired them, but I knew nothing about their personal life. Their role was played for me when I watched them play in greatness at their respective positions. I will mention this later in the book.

Growing up, I was aware of course of going to school with all African-American people, and living in a community of the same. Every time I went to town, I was reminded of that in stores, restaurants, parks, or any public place. The Detroit Tigers constantly reminded the Black Community of that fact.

Thankfully, there were people and groups that tried to do the right thing. The Cleveland Indians baseball team sponsored the Negro State Tournament in Daytona Beach, Florida (1958), even though they did not train in Florida. They open their minor league camps to the Black high schools in Florida. I participated...err started in it.

The Cleveland Indians lead the way in the American League with Larry Doby in 1947. In 1958, they did everything to make us very comfortable in the tournament. I remember one of the umpires was a young man from my hometown, by the way of Bethune-Cookman College name Willie Speed. Later, he became a great college football player and coach.

I was scheduled to pitch in the first game, but I had a bad experience. Someone sat on my glasses and broke them. In the game, I couldn't see the catcher's fingers distinctly, so I gave the signals from the mound. Things worked out for me. I yielded no runs, no hits, and had 3 KO's in 2 innings.

Days before the Brooklyn Dodgers came to town; plenty of discussions would take place around the Black community. They could be heard in the barber shops, schools, gas stations, churches, and grocery stores. My great-uncle David Hightower, owned a barbershop on Dakota Avenue (now called Martin L. King, Jr. Blvd.).

Popular players discussed were Jackie, Pee Wee, Don Newcombe, Roy Campanella, Duke Snider, Junior Gilliam, Johnny Podres, and Carl Furillo. Manager Walt Alston was given credit for making bad choices.

They would dissect Jackie's latest stolen bases and what effect it had on whatever particular game of interest. At times, they would compare the styles of Duke vs. Willie Mays, and Mickey Mantle, Junior Gilliam vs. Billy Martin, or Pee Wee vs. Phil "the Scooter" Rizzuto. Most of the comparisons were between the Yankees and the Dodgers.

They saw in the Dodgers, the hope and the future of the Black baseball players. There were near fights about the differences between Campanella vs Berra, Martin vs. Gilliam, and Newcombe vs. Ford.

William A. Rochelle was the name of my high school. I say was because it doesn't exist anymore. You see, when the schools integrated back in the seventies in Florida, my school lost its identity. Just as in baseball, the Negro Leagues lost its identity in the late 1940's and finally in the 50's.

During my elementary and some of my high school years, spring training in Lakeland, Florida wasn't exciting until the Dodgers came to town. The Black community in particular was thrill by the Dodgers.

On that day, it was as if it were a holiday. Some businesses closed up and we didn't have school. That's right, no school because we wanted to see the Dodgers play.

Most of us would get to Henley Field about 12:00 o'clock noon. The game would usually start about 1:30 P. M. The Black fans were limited to sitting on the visitor's side. Part of that was good because we wanted to be on the Dodgers' side (3rd base) anyway.

We loved to see the Dodgers work out in the field, particularly Roy Campanella, Pee Wee Reese, and Gil Hodges. Autograph seeking was not like it is today. I had cards of my favorite Dodger Blue, but never thought about having one of them to sign one of their baseball cards. The cards that I had of other players I would trade in a heartbeat for a Dodger Blue. My Uncle Melzy Pressley (who would often take me to games) told me that I had a big baseball card collection. In view of their value today, I wish I had kept up with them.

The population of Lakeland at that time was between 45,000 and 50,000 people. A lot of Black people in town and from neighboring towns (Mulberry, Winter Haven, Bartow, Dade City, Kisseemee, and Lake Alfred) would be at the ball park...a lot of them standing outside. There were usually about 3,500 Black people at the field, but not all of them could be seated inside the small stadium, even without the "color line." We would cheer for the Dodgers and boo the Tigers.

Our high school principal, Mr. Lewis came up with away to get us to come to school, and still go to the game. He said that on the days the Dodgers came to town, if we came to school, he would promise to let us out by 11:00 A. M. Well, he kept his promise, and it became a tradition at my school. I know through 1958, (my graduation year) this event was still going on.

My sister, Sandra attended another high school in the 1970's (Kathleen), but by then the schools had integrated, and the tradition along with my school were lost.

In 1958, that's the year the Brooklyn Dodgers became the Los Dodgers, and the New York Giants became the San Francisco Giants. I feel that when the Dodgers left Brooklyn, they left some of the mystic of the Dodgers Blue, at least it was for me.

Although some of the Dodger Blue (Craig, Koufax, Drysdale, Snider, Newcombe, and others) played into the 60's, it appeared to be a different team spirit. Two of my biggest original Dodger Blues would not make this journey. Roy Campanella was lost to a brutal car accident, and Jackie Robinson retired at the end of the 1956 season after he was traded to the enemy Giants. WHAT? Jackie Robinson traded!! What was the Dodgers' management thinking about?

Jackie Robinson was the "Hope Unborn" bridge from the Negro League to the "Status Quo" leagues. He was the first to show evidence to say we have been here all the time. His performances said, we only needed "chance and opportunity."

The man who built the bridge, and helped others to cross over was not just traded; he was traded to the rival Giants, while they were still in New York City.

As a young Black teenager who looked at the world partly through the eyes of baseball, and rose colored glasses, I felt betrayed by the "powers that be." Loyalty was a word that could not be used by management at that time. I think I'm beginning to hear that again, and not just in baseball.

When Al Campanis, a Dodger executive made his statement, this was the straw that broke the proverbial camel's back. Something to the fact that "they lacked the necessities." to become managers, general managers, (This statement referring to Blacks) etc. This statement coming from a man who was in charge of my Dodger Blues? Now that really did hurt.

Soon after Campanis made that statement, it appeared to me that he "lacked the necessities" to keep his job. It brought back memories of the Detroit Tigers all over again.

However, I know Campanis was not the complete racist that the media made him out to be. It was just a slip of the "guh-dole-boyz" network charm. Just as had been done by Jimmy the Greek, Fuzzy Zoeller, and the late Howard Cosell. Now, at the end of the 1950's, my favorite team, and players appeared to be leaving as the Dodgers of Brooklyn. Was the next to go the mystic, the magic, or the blue blood? I only hope that they would remain in the Grapefruit League, and continue to play exhibition games in Florida. After all I was preparing to go to college, and I would not get the same opportunity to see them as before.

CHAPTER II: <u>**HALL OF FAME DISRESPECT**</u>

For the second and third time in baseball history, collusion, and arrogance (particularly arrogance) have flexed their professional baseball muscles of trickery and fraud. They blew the chance to get it right again.

The first time occurred during the early days of the Negro Leagues. A dark part of our country's past. The second time to get it right was from 1971 to 1977. Apparently, the proper type of research was not made, and it appears that little effort or thought was made concerning HOF voting. The third time will end at the turn of the 21st century, according to experts. What am I talking about?

I'm glad you asked that question. Baseball (the major leagues) appointed a committee in the 70's to research and recommend players (minorities) to the Hall of Fame, who had been over looked, or excluded because of collusion. Basically, because they were different than the "status quo," and of course they were not afforded "chance and opportunity" to play in a major league with other people of the same talents.

Arrogantly enough, the major leagues of "status quo," would go to Cuba, Mexico, and other countries to continue to promote and practice segregation, and negative stereotyping even in other lands. They would sign the lighter skin prospective baseball players, and leave the darker skin players there for their own country, or for whatever was available. Available at that time was the Negro Leagues. Lighter skin players would pass for White Cubans or Mexicans. The darker skin players were too much of a reminder of the collusion already being exercised in America.

Such were the cases of Jose Mendez, and Aldolfo Luque. Mendez was called a Black Cuban because of his rich dark skin. Luque was considered by the "status quo" as a White Cuban.

Luque would go on to win almost 200 games (193) in the "status quo" league major leagues because of his lighter skin, and the fact that he could pitch. Luque had the best of both worlds. He also played two years in the Negro Leagues first.

Mendez, because he was considered a Black Cuban, played in the Negro Leagues before and into the 1920's when the Negro Leagues became officially organized. He also played in Latin countries.

Mendez, a pitcher (The Black Diamond) was said to be faster than Hall of Famer Smokey Joe Williams. He was pitching for his native Cuban team as early as age 16 in 1903. In the Negro Leagues he, played with the Brooklyn Royal Giants, the Cuban Stars, the Chicago American Giants, the Detroit Stars, and performed as player-manager for the Kansas City Monarchs. He won pennants in 1923-24, and 1925.

In exhibition games he out pitched HOF pitchers Christy Matheson, and Eddie Plank. In addition to that feat, he beat Nap Rucker, all of this in a 3-day period. John McGraw, the then manager of the New York Giants said that "Mendez was a sort of Walter Johnson and Grover Cleveland Alexander rolled into one." He also said that if he were White, he would be worth $30,000 per year. Why then, is he waiting to get the recognition he deserves? Mendez demonstrated on all levels of competition (Negro Leagues and exhibition games) the quality of his abilities. It is not his fault that he was held hostage from exercising his rights as a human being. There is creditable testimony and ledger about his abilities.

John Henry Lloyd, a Hall of Famer said that he had never seen any pitcher better than Mendez. He was a good shortstop, third baseman, second baseman, and outfielder; however, he was a great pitcher and manager.

Being a fellow countryman of Luque, Mendez didn't get the respect, recognition, or the opportunities to prove his worth accept in the Negro Leagues. There, he was respected highly. In their own country, Luque was regarded higher because of his acceptability in the **so-called major leagues.**

*Smokey Joe Williams was selected to the HOF in 1999.

From 1971 to 1977, only 13 African-American players from the Negro Leagues were allowed to enter the HOF at that time. At the same time, groups of White stars had been allowed in by large amounts from the "status quo" league.

Figure this, from 1977 to 1994 (17 years), a committee made up of 16 Whites, and two Blacks elected only four Negro League stars. Finally, the third time, a period from 1995 to 2000, reportedly the last time according to experts for Negro League stars to enter the HOF. In the last period of time, only one NL star will be named per year, thereby closing the door on those deserving stars like Jose Mendez. Just as they were denied "chance and opportunity" when the "color line" was brought in, they will also be denied entrance into the HOF as their counterparts have been over the years.

From the mid-1880's when the "color line" was established until 1947, it was a 60-year period of time, and under 20 Negro League players will be named at the end of the 20th century. When the Dodgers signed Jackie Robinson, this was not the place to draw the line for quality players in the NL. The same percentage of quality players available at that time is the same as is available now.

What happen to all the big named Negro League super stars that won 309 games to 129 game from the White stars over the years? What happen from a period of 1940 to 1955 to a group of Black and Hispanic stars (not including Jackie, Roy Campanella, Larry Doby, and Monte Irvin) who played in a fading Negro League, and came into a new era of a new league (National and American) slowly taking NL stars and totally ignoring other stars. What happen to the players of that 15-year span? Robinson, Doby, Campanella, and Irvin are not included in this group because they had some time to demonstrate their true abilities, and they have been named.

Players like Aaron, Banks, and Mays were just coming into their own, and did not have enough NL time by 1955. This was my time as a teenager, and I was aware of the lack of Black and Hispanic talent in the major leagues, and the microcosm theory as it played a part in the total picture of the world. Those players selected in chapter VI are the players who should have been recognized from 1880 to 1955.

It is interesting that pre-1947 (Robinson's debut), less than 20 players have been named, and also less than 20 since 1947 (over 50 years), that Black or Hispanic players have been named to the HOF from the NL...a total of over 110 years.

This book is not about African-Americans alone. It is also about justice, mercy, truth, and what should have been the American way. It is a reminder of a people disrespected because of skin color, fear, heritage, and ignorance. Because of this ignorance, "***HOPE was UNBORN.***"

One Negro League star, Ray Dandridge (inducted in 1987 to the HOF) was reported to have said, "I would have given anything just to have been up if only for a cup of coffee." What a statement of great magnitude, and wisdom. He was not complaining about not being called up, even though he could have been, but his thought was on the **HOPE that was UNBORN.**

When Robinson broke into the major leagues and others such as Larry Doby, Roy Campanella, Don Newcombe, Monte Irvin, and Hank Thompson followed, it was the beginning of the end for the Negro Leagues. Their demise brought on quotas, which was a reflection of society in America at that time...one or two Blacks, but not too many. There were players in their mid to late 30's, who were still productive, and they were not given "chance and opportunity" because of (1.) Quotas- only on or two for appearance sake, (2.) No odd numbers please, because they must have roommates to keep them happy, (3.) Older and more experienced players don't have much longer, and they may cause problems, (4.) The American League—We have Doby, Boyd, and Minoso, let's not rush it...and they didn't. Some teams were slow to accept integration, especially those in the American League.

Dizzy Dean and some of his "status quo" friends experienced a taste of what could have/should have been in 1943. That was when the Harrisburg-St. Louis Stars from the NL withdrew from the league to go on barnstorming tours with a team headed up by Dizzy Dean, a status quo hall of famer.

I believe that this was the real beginning of the demise of the Negro Leagues. Four years before Jackie Robinson was brought to Brooklyn, and two years (1945) before Branch Rickey attempted to organize a pre-readiness league of African-American players to serve the status quo major leagues. A team from the National Negro League decides to pull out to barnstorm with players from their league and the status quo league. I always wondered what the pre-readiness league was going to be about? Was it to see if you passed as a person? To see if you could play on the same level as the White stars? So what was the minor leagues?

If the move by the Stars was genuine, these guys had to have the right ideas, but they were few. There were many "status quo" players who said they would never play with minority players. What they really meant was dark skin Hispanics and African-Americans. They were already playing with minorities. When the lighter skin Hispanics players were accepted over their darker skin countrymen, not much was made of it.

They could accept playing with the lighter skin Hispanics because they were more accepted by the community of status quo baseball. In fact, there are stories about "status quo" owners taking light skin Black players, and dressing them up to pass as Native Americans so they could be accepted by the White community of baseball.

In the 60's when I checked the baseball standings in the National League in any given year, there would always be 6 to 8 Black/Hispanic players in the top ten batting averages, and other offensive categories posted. Thirteen years or more after Jackie Robinson darned a Brooklyn Dodger uniform, African-American/Hispanics were beginning to make a dent in the major leagues as we know it today…particularly in the national league.

"WORLD SERIES ILLEGITIMACY"

Who, including Abner Doubleday (it's inventor, 1839) has the right or arrogance to claim exclusive rights of a **"WORLD SERIES"** champion without inviting the people of the **WORLD,** or its representatives? Who has exclusive rights to any human type of championship without including all humans eligible?

My mother-in-law, Gertrude Smith-Jenkins use to say, **"The proof of the pudding is in the eating."** Of course she would say that, she was a master cook. The proof is that today, the U.S.A. major leagues is stocked with African-American/Hispanics players who were not allowed to participate in their little game before 1947 (Jackie). So then, can you say that they were the real champions of the world? I don't see how.

Of course, these "world champions" considered themselves the **champions of the world** even though the world had no opportunity to participated in the challenge. To show how superior they thought they were, they didn't even invite a challenge from the Negro League's winners…not even a "world series" exhibition series.

As I recall, a few years ago we got in the "I'm taking my ball and going home" attitude. This happened in little league baseball. Because the American little league teams hadn't won the championship in a while, America decided to make the little league "world series" for Americans only. Is this the way we want to teach our youngsters? If we can't be the champions, then no one else can be either? I suppose the merit to that is only the status quo players can be accepted as **true** champions. Maybe this is the reason why the Negro League's records cannot be accepted?

It is no more than right that America should be the home of the "World Series." After all, the game originated in the United States. If we are going to claim championship, and feel good about ourselves, we need to open it up for every country with organized baseball. That's the only way to make it legitimate. Offer a challenge to the baseball-organized world.

"Human kind and all men anthropological, come from the same source, with the same potentials must have a potential equality in CHANCE AND OPPORTUNITY."

—Branch Rickey

"Chance and opportunity" do not exist today, and did not in the past for the "World Series" games. Let us examine the true meaning of **_"World Series."_** By definition, **world** means "the earth with all its inhabitants and all things upon it; people in general; humanity." **Series** by definition is "a number of events of the same class coming one after another." Those two words use together have been totally misused by our society. Even the Webster dictionary has wrongly used it.

If we are going to use the words, we can at least be politically correct now that we know what is right.

Webster says "World Series": a series of baseball games played each fall between the pennant winners of the major leagues to decide the professional championship." Of what?...certainly not the world.

Our society through the dictionary even, has decided that the winner of a series of games, (best 4 out of 7) between the pennant winners of the major leagues, played only in the United States of America, and now Canada will decide the professional baseball championship of the world.

Now where have I heard this before? Somewhere around the time when the Black baseball players, after the "color line," asked to be accepted in the game of baseball in their own country. They were already accepted in other countries as human beings, and talented professional baseball players. In the early years of baseball, America probably had (between Blacks and Whites) the best players in the world, but still did not recognize that potential, and the fact that it was the right thing to do.

There are many countries now with professional baseball as a part of their culture. This evidence has been presented in the Olympics. Evidence of this is also represented in the Little League World Series games; they are now more in tune with the way it should be to make it legitimate, and above board. It seems like our kids now have the right idea, Now if we can only get the thickheaded adults to adopt a similar plan to the one in Williamsport, Pennsylvania.

Until there is a plan of this magnitude to include the WORLD in the so-called "World Series", all we really have is the championship of the U.S.A., and maybe Canada.

To say that the major leagues are integrated is not enough. That should be minimal in the minds of major league management. THE MAJOR LEAGUES should be organized in all countries where it is feasible.

Since we didn't do the right things about status quo teams of the past, let's not blow another "chance and opportunity" at the turn of the 21st century. Put in the HOF the Negro League players who deserve to be there and their records especially since 1920. This should be done whether it's popular or not. Not only were the percentage of minority players around then as they are now, but also they competed in an organized competitive league from 1920 to the 1950's. We also need to change the format for the so-call "World Series."

It is a sad day in the life of a nation when a man has to leave his home and country to travel "to far away lands. For opportunity to take a stand, and then be accepted as a man—with a dream."

To disallow the people listed in chapter VI into the HOF is tantamount to continue calling the so-called "World Series" by its wrong name. "We must not allow it to remain a dark mystery."

Two teams, Montreal and Toronto are in Canada, but they are under the auspices of the U.S.A. Major Leagues. Canada has not decided to have a major league of it's own, but to join the U.S.A. Major Leagues. That's fine, but it's not the world, just North America.

WHO DESERVES TO GO?

Pete Rose and Orlando Cepeda are players who gave my Dodger Blues plenty of chills and thrills, but they along with Tony Oliva and a few others are being held hostage from a place in history they so rightfully belong.

The results are the same, but Rose and Cepeda are being judged by standards of life styles that were not used in the past. Of course there have been prospective HOFers turned away because of their actions off the field, but not like Rose and Cepeda.

For a moment, let's forget about their records. Have all of the players in the HOF been evaluated or judged according to their roles in the community outside of the game, of course not. As the saying goes today, "you don't want to go there," or do you?

When I studied some of the players of the past in the status quo major leagues, I am appalled at the selection of some players, assuming that they are being evaluated totally on and off the field of play. I saw anywhere from racist owners, to racist managers and racist players.

The 1919 Chicago White Sox team is listed as one of the greatest teams in history along with teams like the 1927 & 1961 Yankees, the 1919 Cincinnati Redlegs, and the 1906 Chicago team. The 1919 Chicago team was reported to be partly (8 players) a team of game fixers.

Someone said, "if you are not part of the solution, then you must be part of the problem." Players today are unhappy when their salaries are not right for them, and they are unhappy when their personal conditions are not right, and that's good. But what about human conditions? Players were refusing to take the field because someone different from them will be on the other team? What are you afraid of? Losing? Are you concerned about the quality of players? What?

Where were the players and managers with a sense of righteousness and decency? Managers threaten not to let certain players play because it would offend other player's pride, and beliefs about humanity. This was not just a rumor; it was actually done by Hall of Fame selected people.

To examine one player to the extent that Rose and Cepeda have been is to examine all players that have ever been considered.

If we expect our youths of America to be model citizens, then we need to reexamine every player who has already been inducted, because they have set the standards already unless we are ready to make an addendum. If we keep out Rose and Cepeda because of what we perceive as their lack of good citizenship, and judgement, then we are judging them as role model citizens, and not as role model players.

SOLUTION: Give 50% voting weight to the writers, and 50% voting weight to the players committee. The player needing to obtain 37 ½ from each party, therefore needing 75%, or a combination to equal 75% from both sides. 75% is the standard now used.

The HOF committee needs to look at the total player. Take Jim Bunning for one example. I saw Bunning his entire career. He demonstrated HOF performances quiet frequently, but he had a difficult time getting in. Bunning was one of few pitchers to win 100 games in each league. On an average, that's five 20 game seasons in each league. (Mentioned later)

Another example is Maury Wills. First, he was denied "chance and opportunity," because of his size. When he finally got the chance to play at age 28, he led the Dodger Blue to four pennants in 1959, '63, '65, and 1966. He broke Ty Cobb's stolen base record (96) at 104, which stood for years. In his 13 years, Maury stole 586 bases. His lifetime batting average is .281. From 1960 to 1965, he led the league in stolen bases (6 years). In his career, Maury got 2,134 hits. If given the opportunity for 6 more years at his average of 164 hits, he would have surpassed 3,000 hits.

Wills' records are far better than two other favorite New York HOF shortstops that played more years (Reese & Rizutto). Wills was also more valuable to his team, because he represented a large portion of their offense. The teams he played on were great teams because he was the offensive catalyst, and they had great pitching with Koufax, Drysdale, and others. The Dodgers had no great hitters during the time Wills played; yet they had great teams, because their offense centered on him. Under these adversities, these players belong in the HOF the first time. And there are other cases as well.

*Orlando Cepeda was recently named to the HOF—1999.

"IGNORED TALENT S FELL UN-A-WELLS"

Recently, Tom LaSorda, Nellie Fox, Phil Niekro, and Willie Wells were inducted into the Hall of Fame. A lot of talk, press, and information were given on LaSorda, and Niekro. Of course, they are known for their recent involvement in the baseball world, and they are still fresh on the minds of the voters.

How did all the information become available on Nellie Fox, and almost none on Willie Wells? In fact, he was barely mentioned at all.

When Jackie Robinson came into the major leagues (1947), some of the greats of the Negro Leagues were ending their careers, but of course they were not invited to the big dance, which is another tragedy in itself. Players like Cool Papa Bell, Buck Leonard, and Willie Wells. Well was coming to the end of his great career. He played three years after Jackie's debut (to 1950).

The point is it's not like information on Wells was not obtainable, because it was. This leads us to the next point. In 1997, before the official induction of Niekro, Fox, Wells, and LaSorda, and article appeared in the Atlanta Journal-Constitution. It read, "Their Biggest Claim to Fame: These <u>three</u> beat the odds."

It continued to say that these are the guys (speaking of only Niekro, LaSorda, and Fox) who were 100,000 to 1 shots of ever making the Baseball Hall of Fame. It further stated that "LaSorda, Fox, and Niekro came from as far back in the pack as a player can come, climbed not hills, but mountains, clawed their way through <u>obscurity </u>into the permanent glow of a place on the wall of this Louvre of Baseball."

I'm sure these three are very deserving of a place in the HOF. In fact, Tommy LaSorda is one of my favorite Dodger Blue managers, and I saw Nellie Fox enough to know that he belongs in the HOF, the first time around.

However, it is hard for me to understand how Willie Wells was not displayed with the same intensification, magnitude, and research that the other three HOFers were. Was this the writer's way of saying Willie did not really belong? Or was it just bad reporting? I choose to believe the former because of the patterns that have been set for NL players in the past.

If LaSorda, Niekro, and Fox are 100,000 to 1 shots of making the HOF, what percentage was Wells? A man who was not allowed to compete, because of the "color line." Willie Wells really played in total obscurity. He is the man who would **really** know what obscurity meant. LaSorda, Fox, and Niekro had the means, ways, and "chance and opportunity" to "be all they could be" in baseball and America.

<u>"In Mexico, Cuba and other places you toiled.</u>
<u>While honing your skills on distant soil."</u>

—John Carswell

It's like; here is a part of our history. It's here, but we don't have to recognize it. It's here, but we don't have to give it credibility. Just as the veterans committee is there to do research on players from the past of the "status quo" league players, research can be done on the Negro League's players. Some of them are still alive with information. There are Black historians and other resources to get the information from.

As a teenager, I use to read the Pittsburgh Courier, and the Amsterdam Newspapers. I enjoyed the accounts of the All-American football teams from Black Colleges and Universities. Also reports on the Negro Leagues and what was happening to them as they lost their identities, and when the NL was full of good and great players.

It appears that ignoring and disrespecting others can be found inside and outside the HOF. The Negro Leagues are apart of American history, just as African-Americans are apart of history. Years after Jackie broke the modern day "color line" in 1947; Ernie Banks hit from 1955 to 1960, more homeruns than any major leaguer. (Banks was another player who did not need to spend time in the minors) By the end of two decades (1949-1969), African-Americans, or Hispanics would win the MVP award 16 of 19 years in the National League. The same quality of players was also around before Jackie signed, and they need to be recognized. This move by baseball in the 40's and 50's was also projected into our society and spreaded everywhere. In schools, bus stations, public facilities and other places were affected.

<u>*"It will be solved in baseball, it will be solved educationally, it will be solved*</u>
<u>*everywhere in the course of time."*</u>

—Branch Rickey

The window of opportunity for African-Americans for the HOF from the Negro Leagues has only been open since 1971. At this writing, only 14 Negro League stars have been inducted in almost a 30-year period. The earliest to play of these 14 is Rube Foster. He started his baseball career in 1902. As I will show,

19

there were many African-American and Hispanic players in the Negro Leagues before and after Rube Foster, as early as Bud Fowler (a.k.a.) John W. Jackson in 1887. The first professional Black player to play in the major leagues was Moses Fleetwood Walker in 1884. It was not Jackie Robinson. Black and Hispanic players have been there from the beginning.

What are we saying here? That after almost 70 years, (since 1936) only 14 African-American/Hispanic players who paralleled careers with Ruth, Anson, Cobb, Cochrane, Greenberg, Three Fingers Brown, etc., are in the HOF.

We need to be reminded again at this point, that when players from the Negro Leagues met the players from the status quo leagues, albeit exhibition games, the Black/Hispanics stars won over 60% of the time. Those NL players did not win with smoke and mirrors, although Satchel Paige was so unhittable that they probably thought so.

With the closing to the Negro League vets into the doors of the HOF into the 21st century, it continues to look very much like the Hall of Shame.

The late Jake Gaither, the former great legendary football coach at Florida A & M University (a Black school) made a statement in the 60's before the integration of the schools in the south. Jake said for the schools to integrate would mean the destruction of his football program, and others like his.

When he made that statement, I was upset with him because I thought he wanted to stop the Black community from making progress in education and sports. I thought for a moment that hear was a man who had let time pass by him. NOT.

This is what he really meant. Florida A & M University had been one of the top Black colleges in America over the years. Jake Gaither and Eddie Robinson of Grambling University received the crème de La crème of Black players, particularly from the south. Jake felt that he would be losing the top quality division I Black players that he had been receiving over the years to maintain the same quality program, and he was right. Jake received this quality of players even though the school wasn't considered a division I school. This was mainly due to the fact that African-American students were not being accepted at many pre-nominally White schools. At this time none was being accepted in southern schools.

Of course, these players now attend Alabama, Florida, Florida State, Georgia, LSU, South Carolina, Virginia, Maryland, Mississippi, Clemson, etc. A lot of Black student-athletes were already attending schools in the north like Penn State, Syracuse, Rutgers, and other big east and western schools (UCLA, USC).

My cousin, Robert Carswell, who is currently attending Clemson, and his brother James, who attended Presbyterian would have probably gone to Florida A & M, Jackson State or a Grambling type school.

Big Ten schools and PAC-10 schools were also early schools of choice for African-Americans who were division I players, but had a limited number of places to go.

VALUE OF ORGANIZATION AND RECORDS

Professional baseball started in 1869 with the Cincinnati Red Stockings, an all White team. Black players played on some teams during the early days of professional baseball, until the "color line" was established. Once the "color line" was established, African-American and Hispanic (dark skin) players had to resort to forming their own teams and eventually their own league in 1920. Teams like the Page Fence Giants of 1894, the Cuban Giants of 1885, and the Chicago Unions of 1888 were the first teams.

When major league baseball players retire, they sometimes become HOFers, if they are fortunate enough to have the numbers and support. They also become coaches, managers, scouts, vice-presidents, and general managers, etc.

Why do you suppose there were not any Italian-American, Polish-American, or Jewish-American teams? The reason is simple. They all played under the umbrella of the status quo major league...id. Aldolfo Luque.

Black players or dark skin Hispanics were excluded from those teams labeled as "White teams."

Black teams went in and out of organizational structure up until 1920. This happened because of the lack of financial and fan support, but they survived during the depression of the 30's. The people responsible should be honored and recognized.

The point here is that a place is recorded in history for certain people, while another group was denied its proper place to be recorded (id. "Louvre of Baseball") in baseball history. These are the recordings.

(1) A group of a few Black/Hispanic players who came into the current major leagues from 1949 to 1969, and won 16 of 19 MVP awards, and (2) An exhibition of homeruns hit by Ernie Banks from 1955 to 1960 (the most). Both are examples of what was missing in the status quo major leagues. And it is also why I believe that all of their (the status quo league) records cannot and should not be take at full value...no more or less than the Negro Major Leagues.

VALUE OF INCLUSION

Years ago, I recall a time when I was in high school. African-Americans were not important in the news or media, unless it was something negative for the other part of the world to know. In my own hometown, (Lakeland, Fla.), the newspaper was the Lakeland Ledger. They still make deliveries to my mother's house.

The Ledger would not put Black people in the regular news section. They would be placed somewhere in the back (the last section) after the sports, or the ads. They had a section called "News of Interest to Colored People." I draw four conclusions from this: (1.) The Ledger believed that Black people were not interested in any other part of the news, but Black news, (2.) The paper felt that Black people were not worthy to mix in with the regular news, (3.) The Ledger believed that the White citizens were not interested in Black news, and (4.) They didn't care what Black people thought or wanted.

If a Black person committed a crime, say murder, particular if it were against a member of the opposite race, it would be a headliner on the front page of the first section. This is an example of how "hope unborn" was untold. The media today covers almost everything regardless of how trite it might be.

In the era of the Negro Leagues, it was very important to have some type of media coverage, and it was important to have scribes of some repute. People like Wendell Smith, Mal Godde, Sol White, John B. Holway, Judge Norris Coleman, Daniel Okrent, and many more especially James A.Riley are responsible for making this happen. Of course, first hand information is the best kind. That's why the survival of Black newspapers, their reporters, writers and historians were vitally important, because they were there.

By denying Blacks/Hispanics the proper-recorded history, the status quo has caused doubt in the validity of their records, and as a result it has affected the Black community in general. Status quo executives, managers, players, coaches, and owners have been allowed to determine the flow of baseball in America. One significant executive, manager, or player has an opportunity to influence many people, and those people many more.

Let's take Andrew "Rube" Foster. He was nicknamed "Rube" because he out pitched Rube Wadell, the ace of Connie Mack's Philadelphia Athletics, and taught him a major pitch. Foster also taught Christy Mathewson of the New York Giants his famous "fade-away" pitch. Wadell and Mathewson were early inductees into the Hall of Fame. A committee of mostly status quo members inducted Foster in 1981. These members mercifully decided 34 years after Jackie was given a chance, that Foster could now have his chance.

Negro League veterans say that Willie Foster, Rube's half brother was a much better pitcher than Rube. Rube is also considered to be Black baseball's greatest manager. He was mostly responsible for Black baseball's continued existence, development of many players, championship teams (1910-22), and the pioneer of the Negro Leagues as an organization.

The year Rube Foster beat Rube Waddell (1902), and taught him the famous fade away pitch Foster reportedly won 51 games.

All of this, and Rube Fosters' efforts barely scratched the surface of what he reportedly did. Think of what he really could have contributed to the game of baseball. Foster quite possibly could have been the greatest manager of all time. That is another part of our dark history that we will never know about. Another example of "hope unborn, untried, and untold."

CHAPTER III: **THE CHANGING OF THE SPORTS WORLD**

It was during the time in the late 1950's when the Dodgers and Giants moved together to the West Coast (1958). At this time, I feel baseball was becoming more of a business, than just a good old fashion American game. Prior to this move, no major league team existed on the West Coast.

My high school lost its initial identity sometimes after this move to the West Coast. In the 60's, my high school prepared to change to an elementary school. My college was also preparing to change. A third move from St. Augustine, Florida to Miami, Florida.

In the late forties the Negro Leagues started to lose its former self and it finally happened in the mid-50's. Most of the Negro League's top players were lost to the major leagues. In the late-50's the NL was just minor league baseball.

Communities were lost when White fans migrated from the cities to the suburbs, to the West Coast, and the Sunbelt. Of course, this was in big cities with major league baseball stadiums.

Smaller cities had other ways of losing their identities, for example. In my hometown, the Detroit Tigers already had their training facilities in the Black community. My father-in-law, Gilbert Jenkins, was their chef for many years. When they had no Black or Hispanic players (dark skin); after training and dining, they would just return to local motels that were designated for Whites only.

When the Tigers got their first Black players, they could not stay with their "teammates." They had to find some Black person or family to live with in Lakeland.

Boog Powell (formerly of the Baltimore Orioles) had a good career, and grew up in Lakeland about the same time as I did. I knew about Boog Powell, but Boog probably didn't know anything about me. Why? Because Boog and his school were covered by the media. I was the ace pitcher on my team, and my friends did not know when or where I was pitching until almost game time. Not to take anything from Boog, because he was a talented player, but look at the talented fellows I played with many just as talented and gifted as Boog Powell.

Fellows like Oscar Walker, Ike Walker, Robert Rhou, and Lorenzo Smith were apart of my high school team. Of course, we never saw scouts until the Cleveland Indians had them in the Florida State Tournament for Negroes.

By this time, our season had come to an end. I'm sure these things happened all over the country, and particularly in the south.

The Cleveland Indians discovered Jim (Mudcat) Grant just down the road in Dade City. When we played Dade City, Mudcat had graduated. His brother A.K.A. "Swampfire" was later signed to a professional contract and was probably seen in a tryout somewhere.

One scout who was overheard, and shall remain nameless said, "sure these Niggers can play, but who wants to see them play?" And baseball is called the "game of the American people," and "the national past time?" Maybe we need to redefine "national past time?" Oh, and let's redefine "American people" while we are at it.

My little girl brought home an assignment from school. She was to do a report on the "American Indians," and what they had to do with Thanksgiving.

First of all, as an eight-year old, without any prior knowledge or a lesson about the subject, how was she supposed to do this? Secondly, When I was in school, the term was "Indians." I would think that today in our more intelligent world and country, our culture would have learned the term "Native Americans" better from the Native Americans themselves. Thirdly, I would hope that our educators are better equipped, and more sensitive about the initial Thanksgiving story, which would also include the relationship with the Pilgrims.

As a child, certain things pertaining to race puzzled me. In Tampa, Florida, 30 miles from Lakeland, I used to see Cuban people all the time. They use to come into my Uncle Frank's grocery store. They were different in appearances, just as all Americans are. Some were dark, some were light, some even appeared to be White...as are all Americans. But they were all Cubans. However, we have not accepted the light and dark concept in our country. As a twelve- year old, I couldn't understand that. The lighter the more acceptable.

The other day, I heard a sportscaster say, "Bobby Jones (the golfer) left a legacy that can never be broken." So what does that mean? Everybody else should just play golf for fun? No professionals please! Don't challenge any of the records from the great past...they were the best forever and ever.

When Hank Aaron was approaching Babe Ruth's homerun record, he received all kinds of threats and abusive mail. Hank Aaron was not to think that he was as good or better than Babe Ruth. There was so much hate and racism involved, until the obvious non-bias comparisons could not be made...not that any should have been made in the first place.

LET'S MAKE COMPARISONS ANYWAY

The first comparison that I would have made is the quality of the baseball at that time with the current time. Secondly, I would compare what it could have been with all people allowed to play with who really did play. Thirdly, I would not compare two different times, but the same time. Imagine if you will that there were no Black or dark skin Hispanics players in the major leagues? What would be the quality of the league?

Let's name a few since the time of Jackie Robinson. Jackie and Frank Robinson, Hank Aaron, Ernie Banks, Larry Doby, Minnie Minoso, Roberto Clemente, Roy Campanella, Lou Brock, Rickey Henderson, Maury Wills, Willie

Stargell, Don Newcombe, Ken Griffey and Ken Jr., Bill White, Bobby Boyd, Bobby and Barry Bonds, Juan Maricial, The Alou's, Jose Cruz, Satchel (better late than never) Paige, Sammy Sosa, Elston Howard, Junior Gilliam, Manny Sanguillen, Tommy and Willie Davis, Brooks Lawrence, and all of today's players I left out.

These players and many we left out, have made a big impact in the complete history of baseball since 1947. None of these players would have been allowed to play during Ruth's time. Babe Ruth did not play night baseball, and if he were allowed to, it would have not been with the same quality of players of today, because of the "color line." The Babe did not travel coast to coast, nor did he face that special left-handed pitcher in crucial situations everyday such as is dictated today.

He did not face the likes of Willie Foster, Satchel Paige, Bullet Joe Rogan, Smokey Joe Williams, Jose' Mendez, Pete Hill, Slim Jones, or any other great pitchers from the Negro Major Leagues in his era, league wise. These are some of the players (see their records in chapter VI) who were denied "chance and opportunity" to play in the real major leagues, and so was Babe Ruth. The reason being of course is that "the real major leagues," did not really exist then. Obviously, had they been allowed to play together, it would have been THE MAJOR LEAGUES.

We can make the same argument with Ruth vs. Roger Maris who hit 61 homeruns in 8 more games than Ruth, even though they were White. However, just like with Aaron, other game conditions existed with Maris that didn't with Ruth.

I contend that Ruth's homerun record is the record of the "status quo" Major Leagues, and that Josh Gibson's record (84 homeruns) is the record of the Negro Major Leagues. I also feel that Hank Aaron and Roger Maris records are real Major League records. Because they played after the "color line" was lifted. Not only should the Negro Major League's record be accepted with the status quo league's record, but up until 1952 or thereabouts.

When Jackie was allowed to play in 1947, <u>all</u> of the major league players from the NML were not allowed to sign, just Jackie. Most of the other players were brought along through a "period of adjustment," which included for most of them time spent in the minor leagues. Jackie was not the only quality player.

The proof of this is that players who eventually played, and made major contributions, some were HOF players who played on that level, but had to play minor league ball at that time. I feel those players such as Roy Campanella, Don Newcombe, Satchel Paige, Minnie Minoso, Bob Boyd, Hank Thompson, and Buck O'Neill are a few of many players who could have played immediately, and the status quo major leagues knew this.

//

There appears to be a new statistics today concerning power hitters. They are now saying that the best homerun hitters have a less per at-bat ratio. Strangely, in that specified poll none of them are minorities. In that discovery, did they? 1. Consider conditions of the game as a factor? 2. Examine the texture of the ball? 3. What about the stadiums? 4. What about the athletes? Were all the players there who could make a difference? And 5. What about the equipment? .

To really make this a creditable comparison, lets do Ruth vs. Maris at Yankee Stadium. How many balls did Babe Ruth hit over that short right field fence that is only (296 ft.) anyway during his record year?

Maris hit at least 8 homeruns of his 61 over that short fence. Arguably, you could say that if Mantle were strictly a left-handed batter instead of a switch hitter, he would have broken that record easily.

When racism is omitted, we can make a more applicable and accurate evaluation. The game was different in Ruth's time than Aaron's. Players were used differently. Today, there are four and five starters in a pitching rotation. There are long relievers, and short relievers. There are platooning systems, specialists for left-hander vs. left-hander, and right-hander. Some teams because of present conditions carry twelve pitchers.

In Ruth's time, it was not uncommon for a pitcher to pitch a doubleheader. Dizzy Dean spoke of this often. This would mean consequently less use or need for the relief pitchers long or short. It would also change the stamina and endurance throughout the year of the starting pitcher. It could possibly make the relief pitchers lose effectiveness by inactivity.

In the Negro Leagues during Ruth's time, Satchel Paige reported that one time he pitched 29 complete games in a month, and on occasions he would pitch 3 games in a day. The times are incomparable.

So why do we make those records official, and not the ones in the NML? What about Josh Gibson and his homerun records for a year of 84? Second place was the year he hit 74 homeruns. What is the reason that the status quo major leagues should be any more valid than the NML, particularly since 1920 was when the NML became organized?

"About The Real Homerun King"

Aaron had pressure on him, not just threats and mail, but from the media, and from the record alone, and maybe as an African-American. In a way, he had to carry some of the same pressures that Jackie had to carry. What about this scenario? Be a good little boy and don't say anything about the Babe, or his record. Hank probably had pressure that he didn't know he had on himself.

Hank Aaron typifies part of what this book is about. Although Hank Aaron spent most of his professional career in THE major leagues, I feel that he is over due receiving his proper honors, and recognition from baseball, even though he is in the HOF. After "chance and opportunity" should come honor and recognition. At this writing it hasn't been done.

With Sammy Sosa and Mark McGwire chasing the single season homerun record, it now appears that we have a "season homerun king" in Mark McGwire. I've never heard this term until 1998.

I thought THE homerun king was Hank Aaron. I did not know that the "season homerun king", Mark McGwire had replaced him. I can understand them calling it the homerun season champion, but there is only one HOMERUN KING, Hank Aaron. Hank Aaron played against all competition, not the NML or status quo league but the real major leagues in America.

Hank Aaron has only been recognized as a somewhat better than average hitter. I would have to think that because he faced such smart pitchers over the years, his mind would have to be a big factor also. So here we are with the Homerun King of all time. He is being upstaged by a parvenu of stars lacking in the true history of "chance and opportunity" in American professional baseball. We have a new homerun season champion, but we only have one king...that's Aaron.

SPECULATIONS

Agree or disagree about whether Ruth or Aaron was a better homerun hitter. I don't think that that comparison can be made, because of the reasons already given.

We can make speculations say anything. Example: Willie Mays is number three on the all time (official) homerun list with 660 homeruns. Willie was in the service of his country for 2½ years. It would be easy to believe that Willie could have average 40 homeruns a year in his prime. That's 100 homeruns in 2 ½ years. That gives Willie Mays 760 homeruns, and would make him the homerun king over Aaron's 755.

Since Willie and Hank played relatively the same time, a better analysis can be made between them in regards to homerun hitting, than Babe Ruth to either of them. Babe Ruth played during the time of the NML, and Aaron and Mays came along after Robinson.

Let's theorize for a minute. Aaron and Mays came along within 10 years after Jackie Robinson (1947). Hypothetically, how many Aaron or Mays type players have been around since the beginning of organized baseball? How many Bob Gibson, Ernie Banks, Frank Robinson, or Roberto Clemente types? And most importantly, would these players have mattered in the total statistics of the game, pre-1947? Think about it. Would the greatest be as great as has been presented? I think not.

We can ponder why or what has changed the game of professional baseball, or what has had the greatest significance.

Is it collusion, salaries, owners, players, or teams moving from city to city? Is it television, the newspapers, or the times? I submit that it is all of these things thrusting us into the future.

We can say that the owners changed the game. We can say that they did it through big television contracts, and free agency. We can also say some was because of greed.

A strong case can be made against the players. You would think that in an economy where everybody is trying to cut back, and businesses are getting smaller because of financial problems, the players would be sensitive to their fans' needs. The fans support a game where the average employee makes over a million dollars a year in salary, and the rookies make over three figures. Something must be wrong here. In addition to that, they don't even play a full year.

If the owners and players wanted to show favorably their interest in the fans monetarily, they would try to see what the fan's average ability is to pay or cater to the average fan.

COLLUSION

(1.) Sacred agreement for some wrong or harmful purpose, (2.) To conspire, (3.) Secret craft understanding for the purposes of trickery or fraud.

Collusion for the purpose of our younger readers, did not start when a group of major league baseball owners decided to secretly hold back salaries, and/or concessions, or not rehire certain players because of their monetary requests. Collusion in baseball is as old as the first major league tryouts after the "color line."

People were excluded from participating in baseball because of race, why? Because the majority of our society allowed it to happen. They allowed it to happen, because most of them were guilty of the same sin, and/or approved of it.

It would be difficult for me to understand that if 70% of Americans were behind the idea and belief that it was no more than right that African-Americans, and Hispanics should be allowed to play, that they wouldn't.

We can clearly see where collusion was and is a big part of "Hope Unborn," and it happened in other sports as well, and in areas of our community.

Doors were limited during the times of my youth. When I finished high school my options were; 1. A Black college or university, 2. An eastern, northern, mid-western, or western college, 3. Find and a job where I could, and 4. Work for my grandfather, a carpenter by profession. Florida State University (later my sister's school), the University of Florida, and Miami University were not options for me because of the closed door policy for Blacks...a "color line" if you will. I could not even attend Florida Southern College in my hometown. Of course foreign students were allowed to matriculate, even Africans.

When the "color line" in the public schools and colleges were lifted in the 1970's in the south, Africans-American students became more active and involved in sports on a major college level. Then, less than twenty years later the NCAA decided to make it tougher for them to get in school. Thus Proposition 48 was established in 1986.

Basically, it meant that if a student failed to graduate from high school with a 2.0 GPA, and did not meet the core curriculum requirements, or did not make 700 on the SAT, or 15 on the ACT, he/she wasn't eligible for college matriculation.

A student could be given a scholarship if that student completed the first year successfully, but he/she would lose the first year to compete in sports or any extra curricular activities.

This is a rule (2.0 GPA, 700 SAT, or 15 ACT) that should have been enforced from the beginning of any college training years ago. Why would you have someone matriculate in college who didn't do average work in high school? The answer appears simple enough to me.

Long before the schools integrated in the south, big colleges and universities allowed their "status quo" students to matriculate. They were allowed to participate in varsity athletics even if they maintained a low GPA of 1.80 to 1.99. In core curriculum classes usually it meant less than that.

Smaller colleges and predominantly Black colleges did the same thing, but it had less meaning to the major status quo schools, because there was no competition.

Soon after integration in the 70's, the academic situation did not change immediately. What did change was the number of Black student-athletes receiving scholarships, which were previously given to the status quo students-athletes. I am knowledgeable because I have helped several youngsters enter college, who were having problems academically at that time.

In reference to Proposition 48, if the NCAA had well meaning intentions, they would have reinstated the final year after the student proved he/she had successfully made academic progress the first three years. Otherwise, students would be punished and a successful educational process cannot be set.

It appeared to me that Black students were making too much progress on and off the court/field.

Also, is seems that that position continues to be reexamined and redefined each year.

Remeal Robinson was a Proposition 48 student. He went to school at the University of Michigan. Remeal starred as a basketball player and as a student. He was not allowed to play the first year because of the Prop, 48 rule. He graduated with over a 3.0 GPA, and he was a first round draft choice of the Atlanta Hawks.

It is possible that he could have used some extra time academically, or to enhance his chances on the professional level by honing his skills. Did the NCAA think these scenarios out before making it a law?

Fortunately for Remeal Robinson, his skills as an athlete were recognized the three years that he played. What was so wrong with giving him the extra year back, after he proved his worth as a legitimate and capable college student?

If the goals of the NCAA are to make better conditions in college, and improve academic standards, then they are defeating their own purposes for student-athletes.

Here were two basic reasons for reinstating the last year because of Prop. 48; (1.) To encourage students who are leaving school for the professional ranks, but could have used the final year to hone his/her skills and, (2.) To allowed more time to complete their education if it's needed.

I have no objections to a student-athlete leaving school early for monetary gains, because it gives him/her more options for the future, which is what education is all about.

The NCAA has taken steps to keep back Black and minority students who have just graduated from high school with a 2.0 grade point average, 700 SAT scores, and 15 on the ACT from entering college. At least, that's the way it seemed to me. Of course now, before those rules can be set, they have been changed. Do we see a pattern here?

The testing standards have been modified from the original goals. The grade point average is now higher than before, and ACT and SAT scores are also higher.

The student now with a potential to receive a scholarship as a Prop. 42 student, he has to pay his own way the first year, and then lose it athletically. He/she has to make 18 (or some converted number) on the ACT, if he/she makes 900 on the SAT he/she can get in school with a 2.0 grade point average. To me, this does not make sense, because if he/she can make 900 on the test, there's a very high probability that the grade point average will be higher than 2.0 in the first place.

Where were these rules before 1970 for potential college students? And why weren't these rules or similar type rules sought after at that time? They were not established because Black student-athletes were not threatening to receive scholarships by the volumes then, particularly not in the south.

Yes, collusion can take on many faces, and it has. Take golf for an example. Before Pete Brown, Calvin Peete, Charlie Sifford, and Lee Elder won a few tournaments; there weren't defined requirements to get into the Master's tournament (assuming you were White) in Augusta, Ga. The Master's tournament is one of the most prestigious of the Professional Golfers Association (PGA).

The Master's tournament was pressed into drawing up a criterion for players to be eligible to play, when they had not done so from the beginning.

Why, from the crème de la crème of professional golf is it now necessary to make certain invitational rules, which had not been done from the previous tournaments? Why was it now necessary to make those changes when Black players became eligible by the same rules? Another important question is why did the other players participate when it was not right for their fellow colleagues and professional associates to be excluded? Obviously, they were not fellow colleagues, or professional associates, since they knew this was definitely wrong.

The solution could have been, if the Master's tournament selection committee had good intentions (id. NCAA, Major Leagues Baseball), they would have made the right decisions to keep things above board, if not from the beginning, most certainly when they became aware.

For the readers who may not know, the Proposition 48, which started in 1986 was never allowed to complete the purpose for which it was intended. In a nutshell, potential freshmen athletes had to meet so-called minimum academic standards to become eligible to compete in athletic competition in their first year of college.

When the NCAA made that ruling, it was to last for five years, but it did not. A study was made on Proposition 48 from 1986 through 1988 on the ACC and the SEC. The study was done in three years, but it was suppose to be completed in five years. However, it was not given the proper time to prove or disprove its value.

This is part of what the study showed. If we compared student-athletes to the rest of their class in the following schools (in '86-'88), the graduation rate is the same or better than the regular students in the following schools; Florida State, Georgia, Kentucky, LSU, Maryland, Mississippi, Mississippi State, South Carolina, and Vanderbilt in football. In basketball, Duke Florida State, Georgia Tech, North Carolina, and Virginia had 100% graduation of Prop. 48 students during that time. The other members of their class had an 80.2 graduation rate.

"There's has been a broad-based assumption in college sports that we've tackled this issue and won," said Richard Lapchick, Director of Northeastern University's Center for the Study of Sports in Society. "It's impossible to know without analyzing the data, but this may challenge that assumption."

There was more specific information on football vs. basketball, Black male-female student-athletes vs. White male-female athletes, and Blacks in general vs. Whites in general. However, my main point of focus is the Prop. 48 students vs. the other students in their class.

In summary, Proposition 48 was never given a chance, because it was there only 3 of the 5 years proposed, and then it was followed by Proposition 42. Proposition 48 could have had more potential, particular if the student-athlete had been reinstated for his first year upon proving his academic status.

COACHES AND THEIR IMPACT IN COLLEGE LIFE

We discuss college sports and professional sports interchangeable, because they seem to mirror each other. First of all, I view all coaches on a professional or college level as the same professionally.

They all earn their living as coaches, and the only ethical distinction I see is the teams they coach. A very good college coach can and do earn as much as a good coach of a professional team. The major difference is that in college the athletes are amateurs, and most be treated that way.

There are coaches of professional teams who fail in college, and continue to coach on the collegiate level and vice-versa. Our concern here is the welfare of the student-athlete.

College coaches are allowed to break the rules of the game set by the NCAA/NAIA, then get the school on probation, and move on to the next school without penalty. The next school could also be a victim too. By the way, this as happen.

The student-athlete is the one who gets the punishment. If he/she comes in a college as a freshman, or as a sophomore, and his/her coach gets the school on probation for say 3 or 4 years, it hurts the student as well as the school. The student might also lose the coaches responsible for bringing the student to the school in the first place. Who knows what level of depression is brought on by that first college experience?

If a doctor or a nurse violates certain rules in a hospital or clinic that are vital to the welfare of a patient, or causes him/her great harm, I don't think they move on to the same job of their profession in a hospital or a medical facility. Why? Because lives are at stake, and so are educational lives.

The NCAA needs to correct this wrong. If coaches are "responsible" for this wrong, then they need to accept the responsibility for their actions, not just say it. The school followed by the NCAA or NAIA should enforce the proper sanctions on the coach. What kind of messages are we sending to our students? If you are an adult, just <u>move on without punishment</u> if you did wrong, but if you are a student, punishment is coming your way.

Our students are being punished without a reason. Forty presidents from division I-A schools on the rules committee are making educational opportunities for the privileged in stead of for everybody.

One of the biggest injustices I feel going on by the NCAA now is the way scholarships are handled. Big time universities bring in student-athletes from low-income communities. Their income, living conditions, clothing and monetary values are all different from the new environment he/she is coming into.

Schools like Norte Dame, UCLA, Michigan, etc. are big participants. Their fellow students are use to better income, better shoes, better clothes, cars, and more money in their pockets. The unfortunate low-income student-athlete has a built in failure program at this time.

Wow! You're talking about "Hope Unborn?" They are not allowed to accept any kind of stipend from the coaches, school or anyone representing either, and of course their ability to work is limited. This is another reason I support students leaving school early as an additional alternative.

Historically, education was not meant for everybody in this country. Women were denied the opportunity to become educated. It was illegal for Blacks to vote, learn to read, or go to school with or without Whites. Why? Because knowledge is power, and that is dangerous to the establishment, which basically is a White male dominated society.

I would like to offer a type of solution to the NCAA/NAIA on coaches who have violated certain rules, and some direction on the future of students.

SUGGESTED SOLUTION FOR COACHES

(1) If a coach has been fired because of rules violation(s) directed to a student involvement, then he/she should not be allowed to coach at a senior college for at least 2 or 3 years, or every year the school is sanctioned for probation, or finally some type of penalty that's meaningful. (2) If the same or similar violation is repeated the second time, a six years or more probation period than the first time. If the violation is repeated the third time, the coach should not be allowed to coach again. (3) A student-athlete in his/her first or second year should be allowed to transfer if desired without penalty of losing any year of eligibility. The NAIA should adopt similar rules.

The rules that are made by the NCAA and the NAIA appear to be centered on what the coaches did or didn't do, and what is to be done with the school. Hello, what or who is the top priority here? The coaches and the schools are only in business because of the students. That third party (students) is more important than the other two for two good reasons. (1) The schools were made for students, not students for the schools, and (2) The students are our future, and as such, we should take a personal interest in their well being, and stop focussing on the coaches except were it is pertaining to the students.

This reminds me of little league baseball. In the times I have coached little league baseball, I have always seen this particular coach who feels that the little league was created for him. That type of person rarely thinks about or puts the little leaguers first. The first priority should be about training his group, and teaching them about getting along with their fellow little leaguers, secondly fair play, and thirdly about the rules of the game. These are the important values they will need for life.

College is an educational extension of high school. When a coach or a teacher does something wrong in high school, they are usually punished in a way as to not hurt the student's academic standing. When did the rules change from high to college where the student is now caught in the middle for something a school staff member did? The reason they are caught in the middle is because in college she/he is not just a student, but an athlete as well. This is an example of "chance and opportunity" denied in college.

SAVING THE GAME OF BASEBALL

The question has been thrown around. Can the game of professional baseball be saved? That depends on what baseball management, players and fans want to do about the predicament they have found themselves in, and they must define their meaning of "saved."

If saved means having baseball as we once knew it, forget about it. I contend that the game will never be, as we once knew it. I have examined certain records in baseball, and I feel that the potential of today's athletes, and because the game has been reconstructed it will never be challenged again. I call these "NO MORES." They are:

(1. 3 pitchers in a starting rotation
(2. Homerun champion hits under 20.
(3. An E.R.A. as low as 1.12 (Bob Gibson)
(4. Triple crown winners within 10 years of each other.
(5. 9 pitchers on a 25 man roster
(6. 300 not automatic for the number of wins for HOF induction (recently proven by Don Sutton and Phil Niekro)
(7. 300 saves not automatic for HOF (proven by Bruce Sutter and Jeff Reardon)
(8. 71 runs batted in for the most RBIs in a season.
(9. Post Cal Ripken, Jr. & Tony Gwynn-A player spends his entire career with one team, minimum 15 years (possibly the last two).

Players are still dedicated, and owners are still determined to have great teams, but it is all relative...monetarily speaking.

Professional baseball needs to be looked at in three parts. In the past, it has mostly been looked at in two parts, owners, and players. The third party is often ignored, the fans.

It is like starting a school without input from the parents or students, just teachers and school administrators, or running a business without customer consideration.

Almost every year the baseball community is unhappy with the selection of the all-star game. Different things have been tried, and we still have a feeling that the right players just didn't get selected. I know these methods have been used: (1) Selection by fans only, (2) Selection by players and fans, (3) Selection by players, and coaches or managers, and (4) Two all-star games in one year.

Of course the ultimate all-star game might be set up different if it were universally organized. Hypothetically, we could set up sections of the world's countries where organized major leagues existed.

EXAMPLE:

WEST	EAST
CHINA	**U.S.A.**
JAPAN	**CANADA**
NEW ZEALAND	**CENTRAL AMERICA**
AUSTRALIA	**SOUTH AMERICA**
***Asia & European teams could be added**	**MEXICO**
	***North & South American teams added**

It could work, and it would be a start. This could offer a current solution for the All-Star game selection. Divide the selection into three parts. (1) Players, (2) Fans, and (3) Management. Having each party to contribute one third. Let's learn some things from other sports like soccer.

When you make a cake, you must include all the ingredients necessary to make a good cake. Otherwise, all you might end up with is just bread. The voting is now just bread, because all of the ingredients are not included.

For professional baseball as well as other sports, fan needs should be considered in the decision-making. The market source for baseball and all sports is the fan. Any successful business must have a market source. If they are not included, pro sports even as we know it today will be different in the future.

A very important reason for fan involvement is that fans see themselves in the players, and the teams that they admire, watch, and support.

Baseball in particular and some other games at this time cannot take too many more strikes, or anything causing fans to get too upset long term. The average fan is tired of the continuous reminder of salaries of players (who are actually employees), and their year after year millionaire fighting with owners and vise versa.

After so many years of the weight of strikes, and threats, it gets to be old. Fans draw lines and make comparisons based on where they are, where they live, and the salaries they make, not the players and owners.

Sammy Sosa's and Mark McGwire's quest to bring the baseball family of America closer was good for baseball. It was good to see even a questionable record of that magnitude challenged. However, as fast as that adventure seemingly brought baseball together there are other things that will tear the fabric of baseball away just as fast.

Sport fans critics pick up on every little detail. Sometimes it's better to leave it alone. There was a recent play-off game in Atlanta (Braves) with the Chicago Cubs. The media noticed that the Braves' fans were lacking about 4,500 fans from filling the new Turner Stadium.

Was this a sign that the fans were spoiled, and they did not take the Braves serious anymore? The media wanted to know if the Braves' fans were taking them for granted?

All they really had to do was check the time of the game—4: 00 P.M. That's not a good time for Atlantans to go to baseball games during the week. The following game in Atlanta was a full house…time, 8:00 P.M.

When George Steinbrenner signed Catfish Hunter to that big salary, I believe that was one of the early indications of owner manipulation in professional baseball.

In 1959, Ted Williams, (an exceptional player and person) had a subnormal year for him because of nagging injuries. His batting average dropped below .300 for the first time, and a very strange and unusual thing happened uncommon for today. He felt real bad about taking his regular salary. In fact, he felt so bad until he volunteered to have some of his salary cut back. The following year (1960), the year he retired, being the great hitter that he was, Ted hit .312.

Somewhere between George Steinbrenner's offer and Ted William's offer, baseball has lost its focus, and its financial way. Some people have mentioned Curt Flood, and others Andy Messersmith.

Regardless of what George Steinbrenner, Curt Flood, Andy Messersmith or others did individually. They were not totally responsible. Other owners and/or players played in their little part of the puzzle. I submit to you that the demise of baseball as we know it cannot be as simple as the responsibility of three or four people. It is bigger than that. Additionally, the collusion of baseball has been racist as well as monetary.

Case in point; Curt Flood remembered a time when he was the only Black player on a major league team. They were playing a double-header. At the end of the first game, all of the players put their uniforms in the laundry bin.

When the team's staff member came by to take the uniforms to be laundered between games, he took an instrument and pulled Curt Floods' uniform out and carried it to the "colored cleaners" to be cleaned. Curt did not get his uniform back when the status quo players got theirs.

The other players returned to the field to warm up and prepare for the second game. Curt had to remain in the locker room without his uniform. When his uniform returned, he dressed, returned to the field and was immediately booed. The fans, which were mostly White, booed because they didn't have all the facts.

Often times we make the right decisions for the right reasons, and sometimes we keep manipulating, or keep trying to make it better until we make it worse. Curt Flood was not allowed to have the same free rights as the other players, even though the top man in the organization approved of it. Curt was on the team, but not as a full-fledged member. Some people were not willing to let it happen. We know this happen to Curt Flood because he told us so.

I am an African-American, and I know from past experiences the things that Curt and other African-Americans have been through, but just imagine the untold stories since Jackie Robinson.

There are recent movements at this writing to get Joe "Shoeless" Jackson into the HOF. I have no doubts about his qualifications. However, the same people trying to make it a problem for him not to get in the HOF are the same people that created this type of collusion in the first place…it is not all racism.

Joe Jackson played baseball on a major league level, even though I feel the "status quo" major leagues and the Negro Major Leagues were not at their fullest capacity with the best quality of players, because of their separation policy.

My argument for Joe Jackson is the same as it is for Pete Rose, Orlando Cepeda, and anyone else being judged for actions as a citizen. This is not for the Citizen's Hall of Fame, but the Hall of Fame in professional baseball.

If these players committed criminal acts in the community, then the community should render their punishment. Did what they do directly prevent the continuation, growth or natural development of their league? I think not.

Even if it were true, rules for that punishment should already be in place, but it should not be a life time ban. Rules for punishment on players while they are playing should be applied during the time they are playing. There are numerous things that could happen to players when they retire from the game, and each case is different.

President Bill Clinton recently made this statement. "America, rightly or wrongly, is a sports-crazy country, and we often see games as a metaphor or a symbol of what we are as a people." This statement was made in a forum on

ESPN with several sports celebrities. This discussion was about "Race and the Sports World." The president joined them.

One of the faces of collusion today is to deny minorities opportunities in sports management. The president continued that "making sure rules are fair in sports could be a lesson for the nation." He cited an "opportunity gap" for minorities seeking jobs as head coaches, athletic directors, and front-office managers.

John Thompson, former Boston Celtic and former men's basketball head coach at Georgetown University said, "some colleges eager to cheer Blacks as stars won't consider them for coaching positions later."

Baseball great and HOFer Joe Morgan said, "Some of the greatest players in baseball history have been African-Americans, yet once they're finished, there's no place for them to go." Amen to all of that, and particularly in relationship to the Negro Leagues.

///

CHAPTER IV: "THE GREATEST" UNTRIED & UNTOLD

THE GREATEST HOMERUN HITTER

Today, the best homerun hitters seemed to be compared with percentage of homeruns hit per at bat. Oddly enough, when I read about the greatest homerun hitters, pre-Hank Aaron, it was always about the most homeruns that made the difference.

The number of years a player played or ratio of at bats to the number of times a homerun was hit didn't appear to figure in. I believe it was mostly attributed to the endurance and talent of a player. It seemed that these were the two most important ingredients of a homerun hitter.

When the word greatest is mentioned, a lot of factors must be figured in when we are comparing two or more eras. In the early years of the Negro Leagues, and the Lou Gehrig, Babe Ruth era, the ball was heavier. Today's parks are smaller than say the Polo Grounds or the original Yankee Stadium and other parks in that era.

The language seemed to change when Aaron was approaching Ruth's so-called homerun record of 714 homeruns. Day-night factors, and the quality of the players, and the size of the ballparks didn't seem to really matter. The authorities sitting in judgement did not think that Aaron would or could challenge Ruth.

There have now been two men to break Ruth's homerun record more than once. What does that mean?

In America, we sometimes jump on a bandwagon of stereo types such as: (1) Babe Ruth was the greatest homerun hitter of all-time (before and after Aaron's record). (2) The 1927 Yankees was the greatest team ever assembled, (3) Mickey Mantle was the greatest center-fielder ever, and (4) Walter Johnson was the greatest pitcher of all-time. These statements have been used repeatedly by the status quo in and out of the game including the media.

I suppose in the Negro Major Leagues, the greatest was just the greatest in the Negro Major Leagues, not the greatest of all-time? It would appear to me that the greatest would want to have his title doubtless, and could be challenged by anyone eligible to make claims on his title. Such was the case in the **ring.**

In **boxing,** the weight division champion is challenged by every potential champion in his division and weight class. He maybe challenged by the number one ranked boxer, the number seven ranked, or a very popular unranked contender.

If the champion refuses to accept a legitimate challenge on a regular bases, then his title is taken away.

The status quo major leagues, which claimed to be THE MAJOR LEAGUES in the past, never accepted a real challenge from the Negro Leagues. In 1947,

Jackie and Larry were gradually and strategically placed into the league. It would be obvious to any baseball fan, that there were more than two players with great major league ability already in the Negro Leagues.

Every potential boxing champion in his division and weight class challenges the weight division champion. Baseball should not have necessarily had to adopt the same rules, but a similar plan could have been made in the "separate but equal" baseball world.

Babe Ruth hit 60 homeruns in one season (1927) of 154 games. Roger Maris hit 61 homeruns in one season (1961) of 162 games. Mark McGwire hit 70 homeruns (1998) in one season of 162 games. Ruth hit 714 homeruns lifetime. Hank Aaron hit 755 homeruns lifetime. Willie Mays hit 660 homeruns lifetime, but he was in the service for 2 ½ years. Mule Suttles hit a homerun every 10.1 times at bat in the Negro Leagues. Suttles had 99 limited at bats against the status quo competition and 11 homeruns, that's one homerun every 9 times at bat. Josh Gibson hit 962 homeruns in 17 years against all competition. For that period of time, Gibson averaged a homerun every 6.8 times at bats. The longest baseball ever hit in Yankee Stadium was not hit by Ruth, Gehrig, Mantle, McGwire, Berra, or Jackson, but by Josh Gibson.

Based on these limited facts, who is the greatest homerun hitter of all-time? I suggest that we probably will never be able to agree on that answer. To me, **Hank Aaron** is the only legitimate homerun champion. Not because he has the most accepted by current standards, but because he has the most played in an era free of the "color line." Neither Babe Ruth's or Josh Gibson's record can make that statement.

With Sammy Sosa and Mark McGwire breaking and setting new single season homerun records the same logic would continue to apply. Babe Ruth was given credit for the major league homerun record, but I feel that Josh Gibson's records (84 homeruns in one season and 74 in another) were just as legitimate, because he also played on organized major league teams and during the time of the "color line." Whose fault was that?

Is the greatest the one who hits the longest, or the one with the greatest endurance, or do we measure greatness by the quality of pitching each slugger faced"? Just as some boxing experts measure the greatest fighter by the quality of past opponents. Do we consider the ballpark, the bat, the ball, whether it was lighter, or heavier? Is the greatest just one season? Or is the greatest only for a baseball "lifetime?"

The reasons could be endless. Just think, if Hank Aaron spent his career in a stadium like Coors in Colorado? He might have approached one thousand. After Ken Griffey, Jr., we might have a new meaning for "the greatest."

"THE GREATEST TEAMS"

It has been said that the 1927 New York Yankees was the greatest baseball team ever assembled. That team had good and great players. The main two players of course were Ruth and Gehrig. There were other teams with great and good players also.

Examples: **1934 St. Louis Cardinals**-Frisch, Medwick, Durocher, and the Deans (Paul & Daffy)

1929 Philadelphia Phillies-Cochrane, Simmons, Foxx, Haas.and Grove.

I would like to list at least four, or five other teams with equal or greater ability after listing the Dodger Blue.

The 1955 Brooklyn Dodgers (my Dodger Blues)—<u>Hall of Famers</u>-Jackie Robinson, Duke Snider, Pee Wee Reese, and Roy Campanella

<u>Should Be HOF</u>-Gil Hodges, Don Newcombe, and Carl Erskine. Other great players were Junior Gilliam, Carl Furillo, Johnny Podres and two good prospects name Roger Craig and Don Zimmer.

(1.) The 1932-36 Pittsburgh Crawfords—
<u>Hall of Famers</u>-Satchel Paige, Oscar Charleston, Josh Gibson, Judy Johnson, and Cool Papa Bell.
<u>Should Be HOF</u>- Ted "Double Duty" Radcliff, Rap Dixon, Ted Page, Sam Bankhead, Jud "Boojum" Wilson, and Clarence Jenkins. Other good players were Jimmy Crutchfield, and Sam Streeter.

(2.) The 1931 Homestead Grays—
(<u>Hall of Famers</u>-Oscar Charleston, Jud Wilson, Ted Page, and Josh Gibson. This is the year Gibson hit 74 homeruns, his second best homerun production year.

(3.) The Chicago American Giants (1910-1915) Rube Foster started this team, and brought with him some of the Leland Giants. Rube considered this to be his greatest team, and the greatest team ever assembled. Rube molded his players to fit a "racehorse" style of play. Good pitching, sound defense, and an offense geared to the running game. All of his players were required to master the bunt, and hit-and-run.

(4). The 1907 Leland Giants—
<u>Hall of Famers</u>-Rube Foster, John Henry Lloyd
<u>Should Be HOF</u>- Bruce Petway With Pat Dougherty they won 110 of 120 games.

(5). The 1961 New York Yankees—
<u>Hall of Famers</u>-Mickey Mantle, Yogi Berra, and Whitey Ford.
<u>Should Be HOFers</u>-Elston Howard, and Allie "Chief" Reynolds.

Other good players were Tony Kubek, and Clete Boyer. What is amazing to me about this team is that it proved, at least to me, that racism continued long after the "color line" dropped in 1947. Fourteen years after Robinson, and later Doby, the Yankees had only one reputable Black or dark skin Hispanic player...Elston Howard. Some of the other teams didn't either, but the Yankees were at the top. So why have Black or Hispanic players when you can win without them? This is the same thing that happened before the "color line."

Again I have to point out that I believe the Negro Major Leagues, and the status quo leagues were basically on an even par, but because they both lacked the complete talents they could have obtained together, their leagues were watered down by today's comparison.

Let me preface my answer by saying this. I believe that it is very difficult to select a "greatest team of all-time," because of all the factors I have listed before. I will also state that the 80's and 90's have had several teams I believe could be rated above any of the teams of the past.

This must be attributed to the total integration of the leagues, improvement in techniques, equipment, technology, and good coaching from little league to the professional ranks. Talent now is being sought in other countries like Japan, Korea, Cuba, Mexico, Central America, Australia, and other parts of the world. Talent is now being judged by ability, and not skin color, which is the way it should have been in the past.

My selection, if I go with my heart has to be the 1955 Dodgers (my Dodger Blues), but my baseball savvy says it has to be the Pittsburgh Crawfords.

It appears to me that the Crawfords had unbelievable talent. This was especially true after Cool Papa Bell joined them in 1933. We all know (some of us) the feats of Josh Gibson. He hit 962 homeruns, and had 9 homerun titles. In 1932-33, Satchel Paige was 32-7 and 31-4 respectively. Cool Papa Bell hit .391 in exhibition games against status quo teams.

As captain, Judy Johnson consecutively hit .332, .383, and .367 from 1932-34. A player comparable to Willie Mays, Oscar Charleston starred as a playing manager for the Crawfords from 1932-36. Here is a breakdown on some of the 1932-36 Crawfords:

YRS. PLAYED		LF. BA	VS. STA. QUO
21	Sam Bankhead	.318	.342
23	Jud "Boojum" Wilson	.345	.442
27	Oscar Charleston	.357	.326
17	Josh Gibson	.354	.412
24	Cool Papa Bell	.341	.391

YRS. PLAYED		**LF. BA**	**VS. STA. QUO**
19	Judy Johnson	.349	—
16	Rap Dixon	.340	.362
23	Ted "D D" Radcliffe	.289	—
15	Jimmy Crutchfield	.284	—
12	John Henry Russell	.314	—
23	Dick Seay (helped to form million dollar INF.)		
		.218	—
17	Paul "C. J." Stephens	.277	—
14	Chester Williams	.319	—
18	Vic Harris	.299	.360
15	Ted Page	.335	.429
14	Chester Williams	.317	—
16	Sam Streeter	.354	—
21	Clarence Jenkins	.334	—

PITCHERS

24 Satchel Paige—2600 games, 300 shutouts, 55 no-hitters—enough said.

23 Ted "D. D." Radcliffe—66-34

14 Leroy Matlock—89-14 ('33-'36) One year, 18-0

15 Jimmy Strata—76-43

10 Harry Kincannon—15-8 ('32)

6 Burt Hunter—19-11 (7-1 in '33, and never pitched in USA after '37)

16 Willie Gisentaner—6-2 ('32)

Gus Greenlee formed the Pittsburgh Crawfords in 1931. They had great teams in 1931, '32, '33, and '34.

In 1935 many NML experts believed they were the best team in baseball with a .785 winning percentage. This team remained strong through 1936.

The Pittsburgh Crawfords have my vote for the greatest team of all-time (pre-'50), and you have just seen why. As I mentioned earlier, The teams of the 80's and 90's have made it difficult for teams of the past to compare with them. This comparison would have to be pre-1950.

Staying with my baseball savvy, the 1931 Homestead Grays put up a very good argument for the best also. They featured a lot of future Crawford players in 1931 who eventually became Crawfords in 1932. Here is part of what they looked like.

YRS.		Lifetime Ave.	Status Quo Ave.
27	Oscar Charleston	—.357	.326
17	Josh Gibson	—.354	.412
24	Jud Wilson	—.345	.442
25	George Scales	—.313	—
18	Vic Harris	—.299	.360
15	Ted Page	—.335	.429
23	Ted Radcliffe	—.289	—

PITCHERS

*Smokey Joe Williams (20-7 against the status quo).

*In 3 games against the status quo, this is what Williams did. (1) 1912- Shutout the "World Champion" New York Giants 6-0, (2) 1915- 3-hit shutout, 10 strikeouts over Grover Cleveland Alexander 1-0, (3) 1917- Joe had 20 strikeouts while losing to the Philadelphia Phillies on an error 1-0.

*1999 Smokey Joe Williams was selected to the HOF.

"How The Greatest Is Untold"
"Even Among Status Quo Players"

If we were to look back at the top vote getters for the Hall of Fame, and base that on greatness, or the best in baseball, here is what we would find.

*Remember that a player must receive 75% of the votes to be inducted into the HOF, and he must be inactive for at least 5 years. These are the ten vote receivers of all-time (1998):

VOTING %

(1.) Tom Seaver—98.84
(2.) Ty Cobb—98.23
(3.) Hank Aaron—97.83
(4.) Mike Schmidt—96.56
(5.) Johnny Bench—96.42
(6.) Steve Carlton—95.82
(7.) Babe Ruth—95.13
(8.) Honus Wagner—95.13
(9.) Willie Mays—94.86
(10.) Carl Yastrzemski—94.63

(* Note that the players must receive 75% of the voting to be eligible)

Tom Seaver has received the highest percentage of votes. Does that make him the greatest pitcher, or player of all-time? Not in my judgement, not even close, not even the greatest pitcher. Of course there are no African-American players from the Negro Leagues in the top ten percentage, unless you include Mays and Aaron.

Aaron and Mays started in the NL, and because they did, we can say no African-American or Hispanic players are included in the top ten who only played in the major leagues as we know it today.

Even though Aaron and Mays are in the HOF, they were placed there because of their records in the current major league set-up exclusively. However, Cobb, Ruth, and Wagner are there only because of their records in the "major leagues" before the "color line" was dropped.

More appropriately called the "status quo" major leagues. This is more evidence that the Negro Leagues were considered less than major league caliber when they shouldn't have been.

Look at Willie Mays' record and explain how or why he is the 9th greatest player of all-time? Three stars from the "status quo" major leagues era have higher rankings than Mays, and one (Cobb) higher than Aaron.

It's as though a minor league player proved that he were better than a major league player while playing his entire career in the highest minor leagues.

When the writers vote for players, they supposedly have important information about the candidates, and should be aware of who they are voting for and why. They should be familiar with the prospective inductee. So why have a committee of 18, made of 16 Whites, and 2 Blacks evaluated the talents of Black/Hispanic players who played in an era when Whites and Blacks/Hispanics were playing to themselves, and to their own fans and media?

It appears to me that the voter should be voting on players familiar to the voter. The observation could be made that the HOF does not feel that Black voters can be trusted, or maybe not competent enough? Their reasons should be stated.

The percentage voting says that Tom Seaver has the perfect credentials for the best player/pitcher in the history of the game. The voting also says that Hank Aaron and Willie Mays are the only minorities deserving to be in the HOF's top ten. The voting records of the past, and current methods prove the unfairness even amongst status quo players.

Where is Ted Williams? You see the HOF voting writers have this problem with accepting Black baseball on a major league level. That's why the status quo's records from the past are accepted without question, and the Negro League's are not.

In a recent pole on "greatest catchers of the 20th century", **Roy Campanella** was ranked 5th, and **Josh Gibson** was ranked 6th. The voters were obviously misinformed. (See Chapter VII)

Take a look at Don Sutton of my Dodger Blues'. Compare his best records with Tom Seaver's:

Wins—Seaver—311   Sutton—324
ERA—(best) Seaver—2.07   Sutton—2.21
Strikeouts—Seaver—3,640 Sutton—3,574

What was the delay about where Sutton was concern? Seaver was voted in not only the highest percentage, but on the first time eligible. Sutton had to wait four or five times, why? Don Sutton is the 12th pitcher in wins on the all-time list. He is the 5th place leader of all-time in strikeouts, What is the problem?

Some players are marginal, and it might take voters a couple of years to process all of their information or have a feel for their validity. But the info was there on Sutton.

Also, it should not be about popularity, but unfortunately it sometimes is…how sad for baseball. When I see articles such as the one about the four recent inductees, and how three of them beat the odds by 100,000-1, I have little faith in the fairness of future inductees, or the inclusion of Negro League deserving veterans.

Should getting into the HOF have to do with how well a player is liked or how popular he is? Should it have to do with life style off the field of play? Should it have to do with race/nationality, or how well a prospective inductee was treated by a voter or vice versa? I suggest none of these points should enter into voting decisions, but they do.

Don Sutton was not popular with several writers for whatever reasons. This probably kept him and some other deserving players out the first time and some possibly forever. The HOF needs to drop that image.

To recap the story; two status quo players and one manager were praised for the way they fought impossible odds (LaSorda, Fox, and Niekro) to reach the HOF, and that's commendable. However, everyday Willie Wells lived in America, he fought the odds of being accepted as a man without prejudice, not to mention being a major league baseball player, which he so rightfully deserved to be. That chance in Mexico meant money, respect, and opportunity.

"Courageously, you traveled to far away lands
For opportunity to take a stand, and then be accepted as a man—with a dream.
In Mexico, Cuba, and other places you toiled.
While honing your skills on distant soil.
No longer to struggle with respect and rejection,
Other countries welcomed you, and you received real affection."

Sandy Koufax, a Dodger Blue, is to me the greatest pitcher that I have ever seen, and he is not in the top ten vote receivers. If Koufax's record is compared to anyone who is already in the HOF to the time he played (career shorten by arm trouble), he has to be in the top five.

What about Bob Gibson's 1.12 era record? Who was a better pure hitter than Rod Carew? Where is Mickey Mantle's place in history? I consider Ted Williams to be one of the greatest hitters of all-time, probably in the top four. Ted also spent 4-5 years in the service. I hate to think of where Tony Gwynn will end up…probably where Tony Oliva did.

In 1964, Tony Oliva was the rookie of the year in the American League. He didn't stop there. He also won the batting title that year at .323.

Tony Oliva also won batting titles in 1965 and 1971. Tony was a very consistent hitter. He doesn't need or deserve the pity of a player's committee, nor do the other players later put in who should have been there the first time around…i.e. Don Sutton, or Joe DiMaggio.

Here is a list of players I saw up close and personal for years. I did not do any type of research on them upon their retirement from the game. Hopefully, this is what the HOF voting writers were doing. There wasn't a doubt in my mind that any of these players belonged in the HOF, but they didn't make it on the first try, and some still don't. They are:

Yogi Berra, Ralph Kiner, Roy Campanella, *Maury Wills, Duke Snider, Roberto Clemente, Juan Marichal, *Bruce Sutter, Don Drysdale, Whitey Ford, +Jim Bunning, *Dave Parker, Eddie Matthews, Harmon Killebrew, Robin Roberts, +Don Sutton, Richie Ashburn, Billy Williams, *Pete Rose, +Larry Doby, *Tony Oliva, +Orlando Cepeda, *Gil Hodges, +Nellie Fox, *Al Oliver, and *Allie Reynolds.

*Indicates—They are not in the Hall of Fame, but should be.
+Indicates—Recently selected (last 7 years)

None of these great players got into the HOF the first time around. At this writing, there have only been 26 players to go in the HOF on the first time around.

What is going to happen after the first year or two to make them more palatable or attractive to the HOF? What virtue is there in it to make them wait?

The fact of the matter is that every one of those great players deserved to be in the HOF. Not just be in there, but selected the first time eligible without prejudice, malice, or forethought.

From 1950 on, I saw all of those players several times. I enjoyed, and respected their talents whether they were Brooklyn Dodger Blues or not. Yogi Berra and Whitey Ford were Yankees, but I saw their abilities over the years. Clemente, Kiner, Matthews, Marichal, Ashburn, and Billy Williams were all enemies of my Dodger Blues, but I saw their talents, and they belonged in the HOF on the first round.

We allow the "role model" syndrome to constantly tell us how to think. I disagree with the conventional "role model" theory. I believe that the role for athletes is played on the court, or on the field. How to throw, hit, pitch, run, catch a ball, or execute plays should be the role for our athletes. You only get to teach them about life if you have a personal relationship.

It seems to me that in order to be a complete "role model," their character must be known. How can you be a role model unless your role is known daily to the person you are modeling for? We have taken too many things from our family structure, but that's another book.

ATHLETES OF THE PAST VS. ATHLETES OF TODAY

It theory today on this subject is that today's athletes are bigger, faster, and have a better knowledge of whatever competition they are involved in.

Agree along those lines if you will, but I am inclined to reject some parts of that theory. I think the athletes of today are better coached, because: (1) They have learned from the past about the mistakes we have made, (2) New techniques have been developed, (3) The equipment for training is better, (4) Training procedures and facilities are better, and finally (5) Youngsters have all types of camps in which they are involved.

As a child, the term "camp" meant to me going to some type of facility (probably church or Boy Scout related) in the woods to fellowship with kids of the same faith, or do Boy Scout kind of things. That concept has been up-graded in sports.

So forgive me if I don't believe in totality that the big difference is that today's athletes are better because they are bigger and stronger. There are also outstanding training facilities in high schools, and colleges. Coaches and their support staff are also better trained.

Professional baseball being the reflective microcosm that it is has become specialized. Long relievers, short relievers, middle relievers, closers, set up men, left-handed relief specialists, and a lot of teams use five starters, and some teams have base running specialists.

In the past, there were pitchers who pitched back to back double-headers. This was before "saves," and specialists. Dizzy Dean often discussed this many times.

In the Negro Leagues, during Satchel Paige's prime, he once started 29 games in a month. He also pitched 3 times in one day. It's a miracle old Satchel had anything left when Cleveland came calling in 1948, not to mention becoming rookie of the year somewhere between the ages of 42-45. According to records, Satchel was born 1906. That made him 42 when he came up to Cleveland...maybe.

You see, when Satchel was born in Mobile, Alabama, birth records weren't always perfect for poor African-American kids.

Drugs, good or bad would have to play a part in this equation. Athletes have abused drugs in the past few years, which weren't available in the distant past, and have been aided to improve their performances…i.e. Ben Johnson. By the very same token, athletes have been given the proper supervised medication only to assist them to wholeness, and not as abuse, but only to their capabilities. It could be only cortisone or a number of other supervised drugs.

Some of those drugs did not exist, or were not used years ago. They have evolved along with medical technology to enhance sports, just as coaching, equipment, and self help. That's right, players are often using technology to coach themselves. Personal trainers are also popular today.

Players are using batting videos, base-running videos, pitching videos, and golfing videos just to name a few. Some known named celebrity creditable to that particular sport usually provides them with that information.

In summary, players today have the benefit of trial and error of the past, revised coaching techniques, and technology. I will admit in theory that players today maybe bigger, however, that may still be attributed to diet changes in the past few years. Everything is relative.

"COMPARISONS"

There was recently a comparison of Ruth to McGwire. The comparison was that Ruth and McGwire are the only players in history to hit back to back 50 homeruns per year.

When records are established in baseball, it is very important that enough words need to be put in the statement as fact. Fact: (1) Babe Ruth and Mark McGwire played in two different eras, (2) Conditions were different…the traveling, the fields, the balls, the stadiums, and day-night games, and (3) The talent was definitely not the same.

This kind of reminded me of the time when Floyd Patterson won the heavyweight boxing championship. He was not fully accepted by the boxing community as the real champion, because the opposition at that time was considered to be very weak. So, Floyd always appeared as though he was constantly trying to prove he was a great champion by fighting inappropriate challengers.

Let's forget the talent for a moment. Babe Ruth's record and power seem to be always compared to another time and place (before his time, after his time), but never in his own time and place with his own time and place players. This was probably because they felt there was no one to compare Ruth to during his time. Here is an example of what I mean.

The following names of great pitchers played during Babe Ruth's time. They were outstanding pitchers in the Negro Leagues. The HOF has only recognized four of them. See Chapter VI.

***Willie Foster (HOF)**
Sam Streeter
***Bullet Joe Rogan**
Hilton Smith
***Satchel Paige**
***Smokey Joe Williams**
Leroy Matlock
Nip Winters
John Donaldson
Slim Jones
Dick Redding
***Leon Day**

There were other great pitchers in the NL during Ruth's time, but he never faced them in an organized league game. I believe that Ruth was a great player, and deserves to be in the HOF, but whatever records he has are not as legitimate as it is put up to be. How could it be? All available and talented Americans were not allowed to participate during the time he played. The Negro Leagues should only be given the same weight.

*** Indicates HOF recognition**

Josh Gibson was during Ruth's time. He played in an organized legitimate major league just like Ruth for 17 years. He hit 962 homeruns…that's and average of over 56 homeruns a year in about 60% less games played per year by "status quo" players. And here we are talking about Ruth and McGwire hitting back to back 50 homeruns in a (154/162) game season. Gibson's teammates on the Pittsburgh Crawfords say he never hit under 60 homeruns any year he was on the Crawfords.

The quality of pitchers in the Negro Major Leagues at that time was just as strong as the pitchers in the "status quo" major leagues. Fringe players were on both sides. Dizzy Dean also stated this many times. Just think of the possibilities. In theory, if there were any differences in the strengths of the two leagues, the point is made again in theory that they would have been better and stronger together.

It is not fair to the Negro League players to continue to compare the era of Ruth, Gehrig, Cobb, etc. without including the Negro Major Leagues. When this is done, it's saying that we deny the existence and/or validity of the Negro Leagues. They were not important to America's history on baseball in this country.

It is also not fair to the Black community, because they have been there for the Negro League players and felt the pain of omission. They do not need to feel it again. Clearly, this is pain of omission.

Since we are making comparisons, let's give more credibility to the Negro League players…four Hall of Famers from the status quo league did:

(1) When **Ted Williams** was giving his HOF induction speech, he was clear to say, give credit to the Negro League players who deserve to be here.

The great Ted Williams, the last player to hit .400 at this writing, recognized the lack of recognition given by the HOF committee. In 1966, almost 20 years after Jackie broke the color line, and 30 years after the HOF was initiated (1936), he trusted their judgement, and gave them a challenge and a command to put the deserving veterans from the Negro Leagues who have been overlooked in the HOF. They didn't.

(2) HOFer **Honus Wagner** of the Pittsburgh Pirates was once asked who was the greatest baseball player in history? Wagner first said that Babe Ruth was, but after thinking about it he said, "if you mean in all of baseball, organized or unorganized, the answer would have to be a colored man named John Henry Lloyd."

Well, he was partly correct. He started out in unorganized baseball (Macon Acmes), but played with several organized teams before retiring in 1932. This means that he played 13 years in organized baseball, because the NL was organized in 1920. It was reported that Wagner said, he "considered it a privilege to be compared to Lloyd."

Wagner's first reaction without thinking was to only consider status quo players. What's different and refreshing here is that he decided to be honest with his knowledge and opinions, and give a true evaluation on his feelings and what he thought was right.

(3.) **Babe Ruth** was asked the magic question. Who is the greatest player you have ever seen? He said, it was John Henry Lloyd. Now if we could have gotten Ruth, Wagner, and a few other status quo players during their time to make their true feelings known to league management, team management, players, and fans, this problem could have been avoided a long time ago.

(4) Finally, during the years I listen to **Dizzy Dean** as a youngster, he always gave credit to the Negro League players. I feel that he was one of the few status quo players, writers, baseball management personnel, or historians eligible to evaluate the talents in the Negro Leagues.

Dizzy competed against the NL players a lot. Another creditable person of that magnitude to evaluate NL talent was Jocko Conlan, a HOF umpire who arbitrated in exhibition games between the two leagues.

Mid-way into the 20th century, baseball begun to change its racial make-up. Change from "all-White" leagues and "all-Black leagues," and change again from subtle integration to total integration on the field of play.

Would this really change the game? Would this, could this really change the quality of the game? Would this change make the game better? If so, how could it be better if in fact it were the major leagues all the time?

Finally, could the second half-century baseball players really be compared to the first half 20th century players, and could that first half baseball players (from the status quo leagues and the Negro Leagues) be compared to each other?

An article has recently come out claiming to have evaluated professional baseball players of the 20th century in the U.S.A. In order to have a true evaluation without prejudice, it is necessary to divide the 20th century into the first half and the second half. The reason for this is that everything changed once the leagues were integrated.

It is also necessary to point out that from 1885-1920, the Negro Leagues existed, but it was unorganized. The point is made then that how can these players be properly evaluated in terms of abilities when they were not allowed to freely play?

The article was proclaiming Babe Ruth to be the greatest player of the 20th century. Ruth himself eliminated that notion by stating that John Henry Lloyd was the greatest player he had ever seen.

If all the Black and dark skin Hispanics baseball players were removed from the current major league rosters, what impact would it have on the major leagues? Think about it. The rosters would have to be filled with top quality minor league status quo players, or fringe players. This is what they had when Ruth and Gehrig played…a hyphenated best.

Babe Ruth and Lou Gehrig were undoubtedly two of the 100 greatest baseball players of the 20th century, but to say that they were numbers 1 & 2 is unfounded, and without rational thinking. I will accept only that they were possibly the two greatest status quo players of the first 50 years of the 20th century. However, some probably would think that Ty Cobb should be ahead of Gehrig.

I did not see Ruth, Cobb, or Gehrig play, so I have to depend on research and word of mouth about their abilities. I have seen however Mickey Mantle, Ted Williams, Stan "the Man" Musial, Duke Snider, and some other great White players whose time paralleled with Hank Aaron, Ernie Banks, Willie Mays, Larry Doby, and Roy Campanella.

I must say that I have seen a lot of great players (Black & White) from 1948. What makes the difference probably is a combination of time and, different levels of competition.

It's like saying in basketball that George Mikan was the greatest professional basketball player of the 20th century. We all know how untrue that statement is.

Before 1955 when African-Americans were not allowed into the NBA, that might have meant something to the "status quo" basketball community.

When Bill Russell, Wilt Chamberlain, Oscar Robertson, and Elgin Baylor came on the professional basketball scene, most experts forgot about George Mikan. Conversely, when Michael Jordan came on the court, those players were also removed from consideration as "the greatest..." among the greatest but not the greatest.

To some people, Babe Ruth will always be the greatest player of all-time. Hank Aaron, Willie Mays, or John Henry Lloyd not to mention Josh Gibson could not change this regardless of how much evidence was presented their way. This is why it is difficult to show an objective view of how it is not possible to properly compare the first half 20th century players with the second half.

While the expert writers and the expert fans are considering the top 100 players of the 20th century consider this? Practically none of that group has been around to see Babe Ruth, John Henry Lloyd, Ken Griffey Jr., Willie Mays, Hank Aaron, Honus Wagner, Josh Gibson, Ted Williams, or Ty Cobb collectively. They would have to be somewhere around at least 110 years old.

The rational plans for fans voting then are these: (1) The younger fans (12-45) will only consider the older players who have been presented as icons of baseball by their parents and "sports authorities." Very few of them will come from the Negro Leagues. (2) Satchel Paige (the first NL inductee) didn't enter the HOF until 1971, and he wasn't an earlier NL star. When the world saw him play (at Cleveland), he was well past his prime. (3) The younger voting writer/fan knows little or nothing about Paige, Josh Gibson or Negro League players during or before their time because that history has not been properly presented to them. Hopefully it will be now, (4) The average older fan (46-up) also has not been educated about the Negro Leagues, and (5) Today when there's talk about major league baseball, the Negro Major Leagues are not considered.

So forgive me if I do not jump on a bandwagon for someone claiming that they know who the greatest 100 baseball players of the 20th century are. **Babe Ruth** himself declared that it was another man in another league, **John Henry Lloyd.**

John Henry Lloyd played from 1906 to 1932. He played shortstop, second base, and first base. He was what is called a complete player. Lloyd was superior in all areas of the game. His superiority was not only as a player, but also in intellectual application. It is reported that John studied the game pretty much like Tony Gywnn studies hitting. In 27 years Lloyd produced a lifetime batting average of .368.

Part of the problem existed because some Negro League players considered themselves the equal of the status quo players, but they apparently did not want to say so for fear of hurting future chances to merge. As it turned out, they probably should have.

It has often been said that Lloyd was born at the wrong time, because when Jackie Robinson was signed he was considered too old.

In 1947, John Henry Lloyd was doing a dedication of a ballpark in Atlantic City in his honor. At this time, Lloyd decided to set the records straight.

Lloyd said, "I do not consider that I was born the wrong time. I felt it was the right time, for I had a chance to prove the ability of our race in this sport...and...we have given the Negro a great opportunity now to be accepted into the major leagues with other Americans."

Baseball being the "microcosm of our society" that it is shows us what was typical at that time.

Isn't it ironic that Lloyd felt as other African-Americans at that time? They felt it necessary to prove their validity as baseball players, and more importantly as human beings.

Here are votes for Lloyd's credentials as possibly the greatest player in the 20th century (1st half). (1) "If we could bleach this Lloyd boy, we would show the National League a new "phenomenon." —John McGraw. (2) After the baseball announcer Graham McNamee ask Babe Ruth, "who is the greatest baseball player?" he said, "John Henry Lloyd". (3) Honus Wagner stated that he considered it a priviledge to be compared to John Henry Lloyd, which said something about the way Wagner felt concerning Lloyd's abilities, and (4) Lloyd played in the dead-ball era playing only about one-third of the games the status quo players played.

What is really going here? John Henry Lloyd never played in the league with Ruth, Wagner, or McGraw yet they praised his talents. The status quo leagues apparently did not consider the Negro League players their equals, because their records are not used as official records. So how could Lloyd even be considered? The answer is simple. The players knew the truth, and some of them admitted it, but they realized that nothing would come of it. They were right until 1947, but it still has not been acknowledged fully.

We all know what the talents of Hank Aaron were, but just imagine if those talents were buried in the Negro Leagues? Many players' records have been buried in just the minds of fans, a few records, and those who experienced the Black/Hispanic baseball world of the past. Imagine the same for Willie Mays, Ernie Banks, Roberto Clemente, Larry Doby, Roy Campanella, Don Newcombe, or even Jackie Robinson. An even bigger piece of American history would be lost.

The landmark and Hall of Fame plays we have seen time and time again from 1947 to the present would have never taken place in its proper forum. Great catches (Vic Wertz) and hits particularly in All Star games by Willie Mays could not have happen.

Unforgettable homerun seasons by Ernie Banks, and the tremendous hitting and catching abilities of Roy Campanella would be only stories told such as it already is by historians, and of course people like Dizzy Dean. But complete appreciation would be lost forever because of isolation in the Negro Leagues. We have a chance to restore some of that history with a few changes.

"For what were the hopes of Paige, Gibson, and Wells?" Their hopes were that they could be given the rights of all Americans particularly to be allowed to freely play professional baseball and ***"be accepted as a man."***

Approaching the 1999 All-Star game in Boston, a ballot was made for the fans to select the greatest players of the 20th century. They were to select two players to all positions save outfielders, and pitchers. It seems as though we are asking the class to take a test before they are given the lesson. Further more, the class has only been presented with the lesson for the day, but the test is on the last two weeks.

Some sportscasters in preparation for the All-Star game in Boston suggested that the voting seemed unfair to certain people like Mike Piazza and Nomar Garciaparra. It appeared to them that these players and some others (not on the ballot) might have a better career in the 21st century than they have accumulated at this point.

I agreed with them, but not for the same reason. Ken Griffey Jr. is only 28 years old at this All-Star game, and has hit over 350 homeruns. He has qualified to my satisfaction as one of the top players of the 20th century. God forbid if any thing should happen to Ken Jr. at this time, but if so he would probably get into the HOF without question. Any player that has accumulated what Griffey Jr. has at age 28 and can't continue his career is HOF material.

Again, look at the careers of Dizzy Dean, and Sandy Koufax. Both of these great players had to quit because of injuries. I am sure that there are other similar cases.

For Ken Jr., the best probably is yet to come, but to say that it is unfair because he may do more in the future takes away from what he has already achieved, and gives more credence to what he could become which is uncertain.

Speaking of Ken Griffey Jr., someone expressed at the All-Star game that they felt it unfair to compare him with the legendary (should be HOFer) "Shoeless" Joe Jackson. It seemed that they didn't think Ken Jr. was worthy.

Let's check that thought out, and each of their records with three important questions. (1) At age 28, had "Shoeless" Joe hit 350 homeruns? (2) At age 28, had Joe appeared in 10 All-Star games? (3) And at the age of 28 had Joe faced all of the top pitchers of his day? The answer to all of those questions is **NO**. We could continue with comparisons of each player's career, but the point has been made.

I was please to see Pete Rose and "Shoeless" Joe Jackson's names on the All-Century list despite oversights by the current baseball authorities.

As has been mention, the fact that they were not living up to the average citizen's morals does not change the way they played. One cannot observe the records of Rose and Jackson and deny them a place forever with their peers.

Cap Anson is one of the first names on the Hall of Fame list, and should have been one of the first players held accountable for his open overt racial actions. We are talking about more than just how a person would feel about a situation.

Anson did not just express his disapproval of Blacks and Whites playing together, he actually **acted** to prevent it from happening because he was in a supervisory position. But to deny Anson from the Hall of Fame because he demonstrated acts of racial ignorance would be wrong. He was a baseball player, and should be held accountable in that realm only. He was not the Sunday school teacher in my church.

What Rose and Anson did was wrong. Of course Rose denies any wrongdoing. However, Rose needs to be honored as the great player that he demonstrated that he was while people are still living who saw his HOF performances.

If the community of baseball found Rose and Jackson guilty, then they should have given them some type of punishment relevant to the community, or a specified time of separation from baseball involvement. Permanent punishment is not punishment. It is a death sentence, and a sentence not previously used on players in the past.

Players abuse their privileges again and again with drugs, alcohol, and violence while they are still in the game, and the game finds a way to forgive them. Does Darryl Strawberry, Dennis Rodman, Steve Howell or Larry Sprellwell ring a bell?

Rose is being held out of the HOF for gambling. Ty Cobb admitted he gambled, so why is the good old Georgia peach boy still in there?

Finally, I feel that the players who played basically from 1950 to 1999 were the closest to being true major league baseball players in this country, because then all major leaguers played together.

The players in the first half part of the 20th century played in bondage. In bondage first because they could not play together, and secondly because their audience was limited. They lack the experiences, the expression of talent, and the history.

So how do fans of the 90's judge the best players of past 100 years? They can't unless they know these facts:

(1) African-Americans and dark skin Hispanics were not allowed to play major league baseball with the status quo major-leaguers. Even though African-Americans and dark skin Hispanics were allowed to play in the

> late 40's, 50's, and 60's, they didn't really come full circle until the 70's. Not in their ability, but their availability.
>
> (2) Minority players were slow receiving contracts because some teams had trouble accepting them…and then only on limited bases.
>
> (3) Status quo players and Negro League players from 1900 to 1950 did not play in the best of major league caliber competition.
>
> (4) There were great teams in the Negro Leagues and status quo leagues in the first half of the 20th century…Both leagues had great players.
>
> (5) The greatest players from the Negro Leagues were not really considered for the "100 greatest players" in the fullest, but the status quo players were.

After the Hall of Fame committee decided in 1971 that they would allow the Negro League players in, only Satchel Paige was let in despite the outstanding records of many NL players.

In order to vote on any issue, it is important to be educated about what you are voting on. As a juror, it is necessary to hear both sides of a court case to determine guilt or innocence. The average fan, Black, White, or otherwise has not been educated or is not old enough to determine the top players of the 20th century. Very few are unless they have been apprised.

Had the fans been more demanding for information concerning all major league players from 1900 to 1950, the info would be forth coming.

Even if The Negro Major League players were not being considered the same logic applies.

Confirmed Report

In 1992, TOPPS magazine (summer issue) by Doug Garr, pointed out the unfairness of the BBWAA (Baseball Writers Association of America) because of their history to overlook quality players…six in particular at this time (1992).

Orlando Cepeda, Phil Rizutto, Al Oliver, Thurman Munson, Allie Reynolds, and Jim Bunning were mentioned as deserving HOF players. His argument appeared to be the same, or similar to the one discussed in Hope Unborn, Unborn.

Phil Pepe a former New York Daily News sportswriter, and past national president of the BBWAA said, "writers have told me they simply forgot to vote for someone who got in." Yeah right! And they should be relived of their voting privileges immediately.

Now let's examine why each of these great players have not gotten the attention of the HOF voting authorities by 1992.

1. **Orlando Cepeda**—He was a popular and well-loved player with the fans, but not with the writers especially after problems reportedly related to drugs. His record was compared to Willie McCovey, and he had the numbers to prove it.

Years Played	—	HRs	—	Times hit .300	—	BA
Cepeda	17	379		8		.297
McCovey	22	521		2		.270

Finally, as Garr pointed out, Orlando was surely "much better than HOF first sacker Frank Chance, who seems to have been voted in on the merits of being the least important one-third of the Chicago Cubs' famous double-play combination of Tinkers-to-Evers-to-Chance."

2. **Jim Bunning**- Bunning was compared to Jim "Catfish" Hunter. Hunter pitched on great teams in New York and Oakland, but look at the comparison of their records. Hunter had five 20-win seasons, and Bunning only had one. Conversely, Bunning won 19-games 4 times and 17 games 3 other times. Bunning of course, played for insignificant teams in Detroit and Philadelphia, and he did not play in a "World Series."

Bunning was 224-184 in 17 years, and Hunter was 224-166 in 15 years. Bunning had a lifetime ERA of .327, and Hunter's was .329. Bunning had 2,855 strikeouts and led the league 3 times. Hunter had 2,012 strikeouts and did not lead the league in any year. According to Garr, "Bunning was easily as good as HOF pitchers Bob Lemon, Rube Marquard, and Red Ruffing."

3. **Al Oliver**- Oliver's lifetime batting average was .303. He won the title 1982 with a .331 average. He placed 18th on the all-time doubles list with 529 ahead of Ruth, Mays, Ted Williams. In 1992, Al was 36th on the all-time hits list with 2,743. Oliver played of course in small market towns of Pittsburgh, and Montreal.

Garr said, Al was "a first-class player who quietly put quality numbers up every season from 1968 to 1985." He also claimed that "Al Oliver played mostly with the Pirates for 18 years, and a lot of people didn't know him." However, if you are a voting member of the BBWAA, and you are placed in a position to vote for future HOF candidates, you need to know better facts than has been demonstrated by the writers of the past.

4. **Thurman Munson-** Thurman Munson's records were seriously compared to Roy Campanella's. Both had their careers shorten, but when Thurman was compared to HOFer's Ray Schalk, and Rick Ferrell the understanding for today's voting problems become clear. Munson was criticized because they felt that he didn't play long enough. So why is Dizzy Dean in the HOF? Munson was also introverted, and didn't give many interviews to the writers.

5. **Phil Rizutto-** Garr seemed to have felt that when Pee Wee Reese was enshrined in 1984, it helped Phil's chances because they had similar records:

	BA	MVP	SB	RS	RBI's	YRS PLAY.
Reese	.269	0	232	1338	885	16
Rizzuto	.273	1	149	887	562	13

***Reese had more "World Series" hits 45 to 46, and Rizzuto had a .006% higher fielding average.**

It was pointed out that Rizutto was considered as a "whiner," but when Reese got in the HOF a case was made for Rizutto. Both were considered "field generals."

6. **Allie Reynolds-** I hate to think that because Reynolds was a Native American he was held out. Apparently, Reynolds had only 13 years going for him even though he was the "Yankee Stopper" in the 40's and 50's. "Superchief" as he was called had 36 shutouts, the same number as HOFer Carl Hubbell, and Eddie Cicotte.

Look at these Hall of Fame numbers: Ledger—182-107, 25th all-time (.630 %), Lifetime .330 ERA, 2 no-hitters, "World Series" record—7-2, five complete games, 2 shutouts, a .279 ERA, and 4 WS saves.

Pepe stated that there are three main considerations for the HOF. They are longevity, dominance at the position in question, and career stats, especially in post-season games. Let's not forget remembering to vote. I feel that the main problem is that it's too subjective and not objective.

CHAPTER V: IN THE COURSE OF TIME

In 1997, Tiger Woods won the Master's Golf Tournament at age 20 with a record-breaking score.

Hypothetically, let's journey back to around 1945. Let's just say that there are a few African-American and minority golf players with the same profile, or better than Tiger Woods, and some with less. Let's also say that they were not allowed to participate on the status quo PGA tour because of race.

Because of this difficulty, they form the N.P.G.A.—hypothetically. The Negro Professional Golfers Association. They organize their own tours, and tournaments.

Continuing hypothetically, in 1950, conditions remained the same socially between the races. When the Master's Tournament were to be held in Augusta. Georgia, could we conceivably call this the Master's Tournament, or more befitting the "Status Quo" Master's Tournament? Could we really only consider those Master's players as the best?

As we continue with our hypothesis, let's go a little further back. Five years after the N.P.G.A. were supposedly to have formed; several players stepped up to be outstanding professional golfers as reported by the outstanding Black news media.

They rented regular golf courses out, but they were not allowed to use clubhouse facilities, etc. Out of 200 professional Negro golfers, 25 of them deserved to play in the Master's tournament. Is this really the Master's tournament...a tournament without prejudice?

With the invitation to only "White golfers," we heard that the Master's Tournament players have to meet certain requirements. We also hear the same argument today when the question is asked about minorities being hired as managers, or almost any front office position in companies.

The question should be how many non-minorities have already been hired without the same experiences or requirements being asked of the non-minorities?

As in the Negro Major Leagues, the NPGA could continue for years without a true representation for their talents. The PGA, like the status quo major leagues in baseball, pre-1950's could continue to be deceived about who the best, or the greatest really is, or they could really find out. Of course, the missing ingredient here is "chance and opportunity."

Think about these rhetorical questions. Do Anglo-Americans feel threaten by African-Americans, or other minorities? Did they feel threaten by Jackie Robinson, Hank Aaron, Moses Fleetwood Walker, Lee Elder, Charlie Sifford, Larry Doby, or Tiger Woods?

If for some reason, you are not familiar with these names, here's a brief breakdown on their importance in sports history.

We know that Jackie Robinson broke the modern day "color line" into baseball in 1947. Hank Aaron broke Babe Ruth's so called "homerun record," and is the true homerun king with 755 homeruns. Larry Doby was the first African-American in the American League with the Cleveland Indians, shortly after Jackie in 1947.

In 1884, Moses Fleetwood Walker, an African-American, became the catcher for the Toledo Mudhens of the American Association, which was a major league franchise at the time equal to the National League.

First Fleetwood and then his brother Welday joined the team as an outfielder, and yes they faced the same insults, threats, and abuses that Jackie did, but only for a shorter time span.

Lee Elder and Charlie Sifford were pioneer African-Americans playing on the PGA tour before it was popular for them. Lee Elder was the first African-American to break the "color line" in the Master's (golf) Tournament in 1975. Long before and up into 1975, the question was constantly asked. Why are there no African-Americans invited to play in the Master's Tournament?

Even though they were very competitive professionals, and members of the PGA, they had not been given "chance and opportunity" by this tournament which was by invitation only.

It became a growing problem, and it was somehow now necessary to set clear standards for everyone, as Lee Elder, Calvin Peete, and other Black golfers begin to display their presence as professionals.

Before this time, the criterion was determined by a few rules favorable for the status quo members. This time the status quo included certain outstanding foreign golfers…even from Africa, but not African-Americans.

I had a similar experience in my hometown before coming out of high school in 1958. One of the most beautiful college campuses in America, designed by Frank Lloyd Wright is Florida Southern College, in Lakeland, Florida. I had a friend-classmate (Frank Porter) who worked in the science laboratory at the college while we were still in high school. We used to discuss the fact that the college, (Florida Southern) had foreign students even from Africa to matriculate, but we could not. It was all right for us to work on certain jobs, subordinate to the status quo, but all rights were not received by African-Americans at the school.

The founder of the Master's Tournament, Clifford Roberts having already set the criterion similar to the ones in the "status quo" major league baseball by saying, "as long as I live, we'll have nothing but Black caddies and White players." —The Chicago Tribune.

If feeling threaten is not realistic, then why the statement by Fuzzy Zoeller in jest, or as a joke as he stated? The statement about having "fried chicken, collard greens, or whatever the hell **they** serve," on next year's menu. This was after Tiger won the tournament.

Fuzzy Zoeller was also reported to have been heard saying, "Everybody, who knows me, knows that I joke all the time." Excuse you Fuzzy, but not with Black people you don't.

Any normal Anglo-American 28, or older is old enough to know about the history of the United States of America when dealing with, or talking about African-Americans. Because of the history of racism in America, it is not their place to try to tease or joke ethnologically regardless of the intent, particularly in public. Past and present memories of hurt feelings run too deep into the culture of the Black community to even be casual about it. America has not come together, and has not been sensitized as a nation from the very bad past. Look at the Rocker situation mentioned later.

Here is a solution. You want to joke and tease with Black people; you must first be their real friend, not their associates. Secondly, be relaxed, and be yourself around them just as you would any of your other friends. Thirdly, be their comrades, and someone who cares not about crossing racial lines, but person to person. Finally, Visit them like you visit your other friends, and invite them over to visit you.

Over the years in America, this has not been a practice. Don't do "White flight," do stay and fight. It makes all of us have a better community.

All Black people have ever wanted was to be on the same page with everyone else, not in the back of the book, the newspaper, or the bus. What makes it difficult for some people to understand is African-Americans can tease and joke about the same things to each other, but not with other people. Why? Because Black people have been there with and for each other, felt each other's pain, happiness, fear, and joy. Black people did not create this situation; it was thrusted upon them and they have had to cope with it.

<u>WHAT'S IN A NAME?</u>

It is my understanding that Tiger Woods does not want to be classified as an African-American only. Well, that's his choice if he does not want to be identified in that wonderful group.

My grandfather Martin said, "a person is identified by whatever they say they are. I believe that to be true, however, keep this in mind...Included in the total history of the United States of America, the African-American's racial make-up is the most unique in this country.

Ninety nine percent of the Black people in the USA are mixed with another race of people. I have relatives and friends who are more than 50% non-African-Americans, but they call themselves African-American, or Black. Most Black people can identify what ethnic heritage they share with another race, but sometimes they cannot.

If Tiger Woods does not see himself as a type of African-American, then why identify with Lee Elder, and Charlie Sifford as two of those who paved the way, and made it possible to set the stage for his winning the Master's? Because all other peoples were allowed to participate without a challenge from the status quo.

The media also tried to lessen the significance of Tiger Woods' winning the Master's with Jackie Robinson's breaking the color line in baseball over 50 years ago.

Those names Sifford, and Elder are identifying with pioneering into the game of professional golf as African-Americans. From what I've heard about Tiger, he is a fine young man, and as time goes, hopefully he will continue to make good decisions.

Branch Rickey said, "It will be solved in baseball, it will be solved educationally, it will be solved everywhere in the course of time."

Branch made this statement after Jackie was signed. Obviously, he felt that we as a nation of people needed a lot of work on social and educational issues. Well, guess what, we are still waiting for it to be solved in baseball, and socially as a nation of people in America…at least I am.

///

Speaking of baseball, it has come a long ways professionally, and has made great strides toward making things the way it should, but it remains constant in areas that need to be broken. We have left part of our history behind.

Baseball has done little to create opportunities for Blacks and minorities in management. Not for the sake of quotas, but because they have earned the same rights as everyone else.

Years ago when talk was made about the lack of Blacks being seriously considered for manager, and upper level positions, it was counter-acted with talk about Blacks and minorities having to do apprenticeships when it was not always done for the status quo.

One of the greatest managers in baseball today is Phillipi Alou, a Hispanic. He has done the most at Montreal with the least. Any White manager making such accomplishments over the years would be rewarded with such a big contract; he wouldn't be able to remain with the same team for long.

If baseball has a history, and if baseball is a part of the American way of life, it is particularly strange how our country can accept a part of that history, and then allow another part just as important to be modified or left out. It seemed to be centered on the governing body making the decisions about acceptable history. When baseball was played by the status quo pre—1947, it was assumed by them that the game of professional baseball and all of its baggage (playing under poor conditions, segregation, the wars, the depression, etc.) belonged to the status quo world. All the records, statistics, legitimate organized teams, rules, and laws of the game belonged to the status quo.

Therefore, the Negro League (formed by necessity) regardless of quality, or production was meaningless in its value to the total acceptability in America to this point.

But because they did exist, and were valid and creditable, it did not change that they were, or what they accomplished.

When I graduated from an all Black college (Florida Memorial College) as a teacher in 1962, the school systems throughout Florida were segregated. When they integrated in the 70's, my records from my Black school did not suddenly become void or valid. When I enrolled at Rider College in New Jersey, my records from my Black school were accepted on an equal level with Trenton State College, a pre-nominate White college I attended before Rider.

Often times when minorities are being assimilated into the same flow of rules, and under the same umbrella, particularly African-Americans, the rules change. Black baseball was started for the same reasons Black colleges, and other Black needed institutions were started. Negro League baseball had its origin in White imposed racial segregation and oppression, because of the "color line."

If Black players had been allowed to play from the beginning, there would not have been a need for the Negro Leagues. If Black people initially were allowed to go to any college, the need for Black colleges would not be necessary.

A few years ago, a fellow status quo co-worker asked me why do Black people still have the "Miss Black America" contest, and still have Black colleges? He stated that he didn't feel that Black people no longer needed these things now, because they are allowed to participate freely and competitively with White people.

I asked him to honestly look at baseball and tell me that it was the same freely for Black people after the first Black player started playing baseball? He immediately thought I was talking about Jackie Robinson, because he was unaware at this point that Jackie wasn't the first Black player.

After I explained to him some of the history on Black baseball, I decided to talk to him about what he did know. I asked him to look at baseball five years after Jackie Robinson started in 1947, and tell me that baseball in America has made all the changes then it has today? I asked him did other races of people close their schools down when schools in America were open for them? I asked him did all the Black actors get adequate parts in the movies when Sidney Potier, and Leana Horne got a couple of chances? He didn't have an answer for any of these questions.

In the history of America, Black people have not been given credit for many things they have accomplished. Removing these things would take away worthiness and comfort to our American culture.

In 1902, Connie Mack, the HOF owner of the Philadelphia team wanted Rube Foster, a HOFer from the Negro Leagues to teach his ace Rube Waddell of the Philadelphia Athletics his famous fade-away pitch. Foster agreed to do it.

In fact, he also taught Christy Mathewson of the New York Giants the same pitch. What they did with it is history…Hall of Fame history.

Rube Foster was good enough to teach the White players, but he's not good enough to play with them. His total accomplishments in the Negro Leagues even though he is placed in the HOF are not officially accepted in MLB. Connie Mack whose real name was Cornelius McGillicuddy died in 1978, and he did not know that Rube Foster was inducted into the HOF in 1981.

In the spring of 1947, in Jackie's quest to make his own history, it was reported that when Commie Mack discovered that the Athletics had a date with Jackie and the Dodgers, he commented, "I'm not putting my team on the same field with that nigger." It was reported that it was a gentlemen's agreement which the status quo writers did not report his statement.

Forty-five years later Connie Mack still had no respect for the game of baseball or humanity, but he is in the HOF. He is honored as one of the great men of the game.

If the HOF committee can tell me with a straight face that this man belongs in the Hall before Pete Rose, Orlando Cepeda, Tony Oliva, Al Oliver, and all the Black/dark skin Hispanic players listed in chapter six, then baseball in America is sicker than any politician ever was. This is more evidence of standards set by the personalities already inducted.

So, when will it be solved in professional baseball? It appears that baseball is not willing at this writing to make this happen. It is too ethnocentric to the status quo.

Now for a few years, the Native Americans have brought their case to major league baseball, and baseball has closed the door in their faces, or ignored them. The topic here is **Baseball's Ethnological Practices.**

Native Americans have asked baseball for years to ban those practices where teams such as the Indians, Reds, and the Braves are making a mockery of them and they feel their past. At least that's the way it has been expressed by Native Americans.

I am not a Native-American, although I have relatives who share their bloodline. However, I am an African-American and so I bring that wealth of understanding, experiences, and information to the table of reasoning when dealing with racial issues.

Back in the late 40's and 50's, it was preached when I was a child that Black people were not ready to integrate with White people.

I used to here this talk in barbershops, and other neighborhood gatherings. What were we thinking? The problem is we couldn't have been. Did Black people need to do something to become human? Maybe that's why the Clowns and some of the other Negro League teams developed and excelled in "shadow ball."

PRETENDING

Some Negro League teams played a pretend pre-game. It looked so real until fans could not believe it was not. Pretend to pitch, pretend to hit, pretend to throw, and pretend to catch. It was called "shadow ball."

Many Black people fought this theory, but some declared that they were not ready to stand up and be counted on as productive citizens, and hid behind the street of **unreadiness**. Those people are still around today. They have taken another address, but they are still around. The thing is that this type person is found in all races.

Now is the time to let it be "solved in baseball." We have played enough "pretend ball." Initially, we pretended to have organized baseball for everyone in the 1880's...and we did. Secondly, we pretended that it was available for everyone to play...and they did for a short time.

Moses Fleetwood Walker, and later his brother Welday thought they has chances. George Stovey, Bud Fowler, and Frank Grant all thought they had chances.

In the last decade of the nineteenth century, the status quo pretended to organize totally again.

Baseball leagues adopted policies barring Black/dark skin Hispanics players. That and so-called gentlemen's agreements kept the status quo major leagues White only for a very long time.

From 1900 to 1947, status quo baseball pretended to be the real major leagues. They pretended to have a real "World Series," pretended to have real all-star games, and pretended (still are) to have a legitimate Hall of Fame in 1936. The legitimacy of White and Black baseball has canceled each other out. They must now be recognized together, or exist as a farce.

Have you ever seen penalties in a football game called against both sides of the ball? What happens after the penalties are called on both teams? The referee forgets about both penalties, and the play is done over without prejudice to either side.

Well, we cannot play over the mistakes of the past. The major leagues are (on the playing field) for the most part integrated. The "all-star" games and "world series" still need some work. The Hall of Fame is the most serious problem of the three.

The fact of the matter is that pre-1947, the status quo major leagues' "World Series" was always White, and the Negro Leagues' "World Series" was always Black and Hispanic, and so were the "all-star" games.

Some of the greatest players of the game played during yesteryear, but their performances and deeds were mostly recorded in the memories of the ones who saw them play. Should it remain that way? Should it remain a mystery, or should it be placed in its proper place with the counterpart stars of that time?

A great player made this statement some years ago. ***"There's a catcher that <u>any</u> big league club would like to buy for $200,000, his name is Gibson (Josh Gibson). He can do everything, he can hit a ball a mile, and he catches so easy, he might as well be in a rocking chair. He throws like a rifle. Too bad this Gibson is a colored fellow."***

—Walter Johnson

Is it too bad he was born Black, or too bad for the status quo teams, because they felt the need to ban Black/dark skin Hispanic players? Or is it too bad for Gibson whose talents were finally recognized, and placed in the HOF years later?

Gibson was often called the "Black Babe Ruth," but there were a lot of people who thought that Ruth should have been called the White Josh Gibson.

Gibson's teammates said when a pitcher got two strikes on Josh; the pitcher was in the hole, not Josh.

"What is the matter with baseball? Plain prejudice, that's all."

—The Chicago Defender

Yes, I say that the "course of time" is now. The Black/Hispanic players of the Negro Leagues have been ignored long enough.

They are not just ignored for their rightful place in HOF recognition, but throughout baseball in general. All of the records of the Negro Leagues should be maintained as a part of American history just as the records of the status quo pre-1947 are maintained.

"In the course of time," the right thing to do is to give equal time, place, and recognition to both leagues. The type of person to oppose this is probably the same type that opposed it initially.

The status quo teams proved who they were to the fans, writers, historians and critics they played for. The Negro League players proved beyond any doubt that they belonged in the big time to their fans, writers, historians, and critics. Both of them proved to each other their worth in over 400 games they played together (exhibition games). The score? Status quo 129 wins, and the NL 309 wins.

The status quo players seemed to have felt that they lived and played in a different world, and a lot of them acted that way.

Take Yankee Outfielder Jake Powell who played some years ago. When asked how he kept in shape during off-season. He replied, "by cracking niggers over the head as a policeman back home in Ohio."

The Atlanta Braves, my current favorite team has ignored the cries of the Native Americans to change their mascot or at least modify it. Other teams and schools throughout America have done the same.

The Cleveland Indians was one of the first teams to show concern for African-Americans when they signed Larry Doby to play for them. I know their concern first hand from participating in the Florida State Negro Tournament in high school.

The Washington Redskins was one of the last teams in the National Football League to integrate. Bobby Mitchell was one of the first African-Americans, if not the first to play with the Redskins. They still use the "Redskins" mascot.

The Cincinnati Reds, formerly known as the Redlegs, switched their mascot from the "Redlegs" to Native Americans, "Reds." They also use the color. Over the years, they allowed ethnic changing of their name. Their fans at games also illustrate this. This has filtered down to colleges, and high schools (Florida State Seminoles is an example).

In college and high school, our young people have impressionable minds and are looking for the older generation to help them make this a better world for all of us.

The Atlanta Braves, Cincinnati Reds, Cleveland Indians, and the Washington Redskins need to show spirit of humanity, and respect the rights of others that have subtly been thrusted upon us. I have admired the Atlanta and Cleveland Organizations for years, but they need to seriously consider what they are doing, or at least compromise.

Ironically, in 1945, Branch Rickey in his quest to do what he thought was right, organized the United States baseball League. The purpose of this league was to set up a new league for Black players...kind of farm league of Black players for the major league teams to draw from.

The name of the Brooklyn Dodgers new league team was the Brooklyn Brown Dodgers, but that plan did not work. Some teams were a lot like the Detroit Tigers, who didn't have the foresight to integrate, so they didn't participate in the new plan. Not that this was the best plan, but it was a plan.

The idea probably was thought to be a good one at the time. Branch Rickey was trying to do something even if it wasn't **THE** right thing to do. This was pre-Jackie and Branch was looking to do the right thing.

It is evident that over 50 years ago, Branch Rickey had insight concerning the way things should be. Now having said that, let's look at one of the last things he said.

__"Posterity will look back upon what we are doing today on our domestic issues here. They'll look back upon it with incredulity, and they will wonder what the issue was all about. It will be solved everywhere in the course of time."__

It would appear to me that the most logical thing to do would have been to consult with former players, managers, coaches, owners, writers, and historians who covered the Negro Leagues about the potential or prospective players for the next step.

Major league baseball continues to improve and have eliminated obstacles, but on the dawn of the 21st century, it is **"the course of time."**

It is time to make the "World Series" legitimate and true to its name. It is now time to make the "Hall of Fame" more than the Hall of Shame. It is time for the HOF to abide by its own standards, and change the inductee voting rules because they are unfair.

It is past time to enter the Negro League records into all records, and it is incongruous to keep any of the Negro League players or participants mentioned in chapter six out the Hall of Fame of American professional baseball. Failure to do so makes any of those names suspect, because they are not true to what they say they are.

Racist attitudes in team mascots also need to be dropped. People who are not victims of racial discrimination have little or no understanding of what it's like to be dehumanized in that way. If they are doing the dehumanizing, they are not sensitive to their victims no matter how subtle it may be.

We can say that the Negro Leagues and its players are in the past, and we have already placed a few of **"them"** in the HOF, so why bother? We should bother because it's the right thing to do. Secondly, because African-American history is American history.

Thirdly, the NL has a lot of history, and there already exists a lack of true African-American history known by all Americans.

The issue of concern here is about making baseball the international All-American sport it was meant to be. It was started professionally in the 1860's, and introduced to Latin American countries particularly Cuba in the late 1800's.

Negro League players in a series of All-Star games introduced baseball to Japan in 1927. In 1934, the Kansas City Monarchs toured the Orient going to Japan, Hawaii, Philippine Islands, and Hong Kong.

African-Americans had a very important role in introducing baseball in Latin America, Puerto Rico, Mexico, Dominican Republic, and the Orient. The role of the Black players as ambassadors to other countries has been in place early in the history of baseball. These facts should be known by all of our young people.

Admittedly, it was not always as a role of good will, but nevertheless, it was influence and exposure. Influence and exposure were components that the Negro League players needed themselves but didn't get in their own country. It happened then, and it is still happening today.

Despite many obstacles, the Negro League players benefited. *"In Mexico, Cuba, and other places you toiled, While honing your skills on distant soil."* No *longer to struggle with respect and rejection, Other countries welcomed you, and you received real affection."*

Part of that welcome was to be accepted as a big league ball player. However, in spite of that good service for the NL baseball players in other countries, they did not get the treatment as the status quo players. That is a part of our history, which will be lost forever along with any monetary values.

I propose that the current "World Series" should be called the North American Champion Series.

Until the major leagues of this country, encompasses the major leagues of all other feasible countries, it cannot conceivably use the "World Series" name and carry its true meaning.

A big part of our responsibility and history is teaching our young people. Is it right to continue to teach our young people wrong once we have come into the knowledge of the truth? I want closure for the problems, which have influenced and changed our thinking and actions in a negative societal way.

Someone said, "all that is necessary for evil to triumph is for good men to do nothing." In my research, I've learned that some "good men" did some good things off the field to make a difference. I also learned that some "good men" off the field did nothing to make a difference, or little to change it. The key words here are "good men."

"Good men" have good intentions, and they find a way to demonstrate those intentions, whether they are popular or not. Sometimes, that means going against the majority, the team, or whose popular in what they do, or say.

I considered Branch Rickey to have been a "good man." However, he was not always the good man he turned out to be. He was the general manager in charge of the 1934 Cardinals.

They are considered to be one of the greatest teams of all times, and they probably were. But they, like the other status quo teams at that time, played under a racist umbrella. An umbrella of "Whites Only" players on the fields, off the field, at the water cooler, or in the restrooms. Signs I saw too much of as a child, and young adult.

An umbrella of "Whites Only" in the stands to freely see them play. An umbrella of "Whites Only" teams to play against organizationally.

Somewhere between that 1934 Cardinals "Gas House Gang" team, and the Brooklyn Dodgers (Bums) of the 40's and 50's, Branch became the changed good man that we saw later.

There were other non-minorities, who were good people at that time, and they did not wait until the end of the war to fight racism and stand up for justice, and what they thought was right.

People like J. L. Wilkinson, Walter Schlichter, Effa Manley, and her husband Abe, and Jess McMahon.

J. L. Wilkinson was a White owner of a Black team. Any White owner who has done as much for a status quo team and the game of baseball is already in the major league HOF. Let's not forget, what J. L. Wilkinson did, did not just benefit the Negro Leagues, it enhanced all of baseball.

From the portable lights for night baseball, to the stars he was responsible for sending to the major leagues. Wilkinson was responsible for sending Jackie Robinson, Satchel Paige, Elston Howard, and Ernie Banks (just to name a few) to the next level.

Schlichter, Manley, and McMahon were owners/officers who kept the dream alive, and non-African Americans who made it possible. They are discussed in Chapter VI.

Today, if the players collectively feel in any team sport that enough things are not right, they strike. In the days of my youth, players would strike out by reporting to camp late. I remember one year when Sandy Koufax, and Don Drysdale held out together over salary disputes.

If the majority of the status quo players had taken a stand for justice, truth, and the real American way, the need for this story would not have to be told. Lives would have changed.

CHAPTER VI; WHO ELSE SHOULD BE IN THE HOF FROM THE NEGRO LEAGUES AND WHY? (I MADE THESE SELECTIONS IN 1997)

That is a great and challenging question. I am sure that the HOF selection group, which was appointed for that purpose for the second time in 1979 did what they felt they could do under limited circumstances. Of course, I feel that the mix of that committee was not appropriately selected, nor were they well informed.

To effectively separate the great Negro League players from the good Negro League players of the past is only one part of the job. The second part of the job is whatever criteria was used by the committee(s) of the past, cannot be used again because they did not work.

I also believe that there has to be four categories to properly evaluate HOF qualities from the Negro Leagues. Those areas are:

(1.) For the Negro League player who played exclusively in the Negro Leagues.

(2.) For the Negro League player who split his times between the Negro Leagues and the status quo leagues, not getting full recognition, and could not combine his efforts through no fault of his own...possibly spent unwarranted time in the minor leagues (transition time).

(3.) Negro League player who demonstrated HOF qualities in a short span of time because of injuries, early death, or denied "chance and opportunity."

(4.) Finally, for owners, officers, managers, contributors, or administrators who demonstrated exceptional abilities for the literal survival of the Negro Leagues, and made great contributions toward that end.

Remember, *Branch Rickey* said that a player **"must have a potential equality in chance and opportunity."** I have considered this theme with each player I selected, and I feel very strongly that this has to be the crux of the matter from players/participants of the Negro Leagues.

It is the "course of time" for what I call the caught in the middle HOFers, or twilight zone HOFers. Number two refers to NL players who did not get enough show time, or quality time in the NL, or the merging status quo major leagues from the mid-1940's to the early 1950's.

Although some of the players played in the major leagues, they were still deprived of time, and did not have freedom to totally move up, and make a **clean** transition. The late 40's and early 50's caught them in the "twilight zone" of baseball…not enough time in either league.

Players like Larry Doby (recently named to the HOF), Don Newcombe, Minnie Minoso, Elston Howard, and Bob Boyd fit into that zone, but apparently the committee, which should have been very special was not impressed about their special situation. **Ray Dandridge,** a HOFer, fits into this category, but he some how got in.

This is why a special committee should be selected in the first place. Monte Irvin fits in with this group, but apparently he showed them enough of whatever they were looking for in a HOF candidate…Not that Irvin doesn't belong because he certainly does. I saw him personally in New York.

Some players were dramatized, or met with uncomfortable situations, i.e. Curt Flood, but others met the challenge, and made the adjustment.

Some authorities felt that a "period of adjustment" should have been granted in the minor leagues like with Robinson, while others felt that by sending them to the minor leagues, it placed doubt and effected their sense of direction and confidence that they had while playing in the Negro Leagues.

Minoso is HOF material. What happen to his consideration? He had endurance and a lifetime batting average of .298 in the major leagues for 15 true years. He led the league in stolen bases for his first three years, and played for a lot of teams because he had to.

Larry Doby is HOF material. What took them so long? Doby's transfer supports the theory (which is the one I believe) that says the NML players who were veterans did not need to descend to the minor league level for the most part, but most of them who signed were sent anyway. Doby along with Ernie Banks did not experience that, and they proved that it was not necessary.

Somehow, I get the feeling that Newcombe, Wills, and Hodges are not in because the Dodgers started this snowball. I saw all of these Dodgers play and Larry Doby. They were not just good players they were great players. I have found that some players were popular rather than very good, and that is why they got in.

There are players in the HOF with statistics not equal to Doby's. How can the pioneer of the Black players of the American League initially be denied his rightful place after the career he had?

One factor not figured in with Doby, as with Robinson and the early NL players is the racism. To over come that is a big burden to carry with other duties.

While Jackie initiated this process, Larry experienced a lot of the same problems…maybe more, because the teams in the American League were not receptive to Blacks, not that all the teams in the National League were either. But Branch Rickey was a kind of guardian toward that end.

The racism in itself is enough to cut down on performances. Players have lost confidence in things such as changing positions, or concentrating on the their fielding more, or hitting the way coaches wanted them to, not to mention racism.

Doby and Satchel Paige were instrumental in leading the Cleveland team to a pennant. In evaluating the talents of Larry Doby, Don Newcombe, Minnie Orestes Minoso, Bob Boyd, Hank Thompson, James Gilliam, and Joe Black, let's remember a very important fact.

There were no fringe Black players sitting around on the bench with a .200 BA. There weren't any mediocre Black pitchers sitting around in the bullpen to mop up games. Those positions already belonged to the status quo players, and each team had them.

This also supports the theory I mentioned earlier in the book, that a certain percentage of status quo fringe players existed on every team in the days of the Negro Leagues.

To removed those fringe players hypothetically, and replace them with top Black/dark skin Hispanic stars would have/should have been the ideal teams for America. Because this never happen, "We'll not let them forget. We should teach our own history." We cannot and should not allow the caught in the middle HOFers to go without the recognition they were denied. It wasn't their fault, but they have appeared to be left out. To make this right, they need the recognition from the game of American major league baseball.

One of the biggest problems was the slow integration of the American League. Nearly all of the Black/dark Hispanics were big time players…they had to be. Ernie Banks in Chicago, Hank Aaron in Milwaukee, Roberto Clemente in Pittsburgh, Frank Robinson in Cincinnati, and Willie Mays and Monte Irvin in New York.

Most of the Black stars were going to the National League. In 1955, the New York Yankees finally allowed Elston Howard to play, which prompted Casey Stengel, the HOF manager to say, **"they gave me the only nigger that can't run."** Think about starting your career in a new league playing under those conditions, and the manager is the one who says it, not the players.

Despite the position of the American League teams, Black/Hispanics stars made the National League a stronger league with a few stars. This reluctance by the America League teams helped to create a need for the unborn, untold, and unknown story. This reluctance by the American League, and some National League teams caused us not to see the true value of some very talented players. This reluctance by the supposedly "integrated" major leagues possibly caused the lack of development of future Hall of Famers, and possibly some other good players.

The following lists represent persons responsible for the development of Black/Hispanic baseball, the Negro Leagues, and outstanding achievements as players, pioneer players of some repute, owners, founders, managers or officers deserving of HOF recognition with goals already set by current HOFers, some non-African Americans. Remember that Negro League seasons averaged only about 55 games a season.

CATEGORY I
Exclusively Negro League Players

1.) Bankhead, Samuel Howard (Sam)
Active From: 1930-50 Positions: **SS,CF,2B,LF,**3B.P.
Teams: Birmingham Black Barons, Nashville Elite Giants, Louisville Black Caps, K. C. Monarchs, Pittsburgh Crawfords, Memphis Red Sox, Toledo Crawfords, Homestead Grays.

Bankhead was an outstanding fielder who had a wide range and great hands. He was called a player's player. He was elected to seven East-West all-star teams. He excelled at whatever position he played.

Sam was an integral part of the great Pittsburgh Crawfords in the mid-30's, and the Homestead Gray's dynasty. The years the Crawfords had the great teams, Sam hit .354, .324, and .324 through 1936. Sam had 21 years in the Negro Leagues.

Sam had a lifetime B. A. of .318 in the Negro Leagues, and a .342 average in exhibition games against the status quo as he completed 21 years. He definitely belongs in the HOF.

2.) Beckwith, John
Active From: 1916-38 Positions: **SS,3B, C,** OF, IB, 2B, P, Manager
Teams: Montgomery Grey Sox, Chicago Union Giants, Chicago Giants, Havana Stars, Chicago American Giants, Baltimore Black Sox, Harrisburg Giants, Homestead Grays, New York Lincoln Giants, Atlantic Bacharach Giants, Newark Browns, New York Black Yankees, Newark Dodgers, Palmer House Indians, Brooklyn Royal Giants.

Beckwith was a right-handed hitter with great power. He had a passion for hitting prodigious homeruns. John was the first player to hit a ball out of Crosley Field (1921) in Cincinnati, and he hit a ball in Washington D. C. 460 feet and 40ft. high above the wall. Beckwith was in demand as a player by Rube Foster and Cum Posey who owned the Homestead Grays.

When Beckwith was in his prime, his peers regarded him as one of the top players, He ended his NL career with an average of .366, and .337 in exhibition games against the status quo.

John's bat was what separated him from other players. Ben Taylor who managed him called him a "demon at bat." In 1924 for Cum Posey's Grays, he hit .452, had 40 homeruns against all competition, and hit .403 inter-league. In 1925, he hit .402 and finished 2nd in homeruns.

In 1926, with the Black Sox again he hit .361. In 1927, now with the Harrisburg Giants, he hit .355, and finished 2nd again in homeruns, but this time he hit 72. In 1928, he was back with the Giants, and hit only 54 homeruns this time.

Beckwith continued for 22 years to have a great career. He belongs in the HOF.

3.) <u>Brewer, Chester Arthur (Chet)</u>
Active From: 1925-48 Position: **<u>P</u>**
Teams: Kansas City Monarchs, Washington Pilots, Brooklyn Royal Giants, Bismark, New York Cubans, Philadelphia Stars, Cleveland Buckeyes, and the Chicago American Giants.

Chet Brewer was a great pitcher with a tremendous repertoire of pitches. He learned his craft from people like "Double Duty" Radcliffe, and Emory Osborne. He pitched in Black baseball for 24 years.

The second year Chet had in 1926 was his first great season. He hooked up with Bullet Joe Rogan (HOF) to help the K. C. Monarchs capture the first half of the Negro League Championship. He is credited with 20 wins for that year.

In 1929, he was 17-3 and pitched the Monarchs to the Negro League National League pennant. Some experts believed this was his best year when he also had 31 scoreless innings.

The records show that Chet won 30 games or more in 1930, 1933, and 1934. In 1934, he won 16 games in a row for the Monarchs.

In 1937 to 1939, he spent time in that **"far away land."** First, to the Dominican where he tossed a one hitter against Satchel Paige and the Ciudad Truillo. Josh Gibson and Cool Papa Bell were also apart of the team.

In 1938, Chet became the first Black American to play in Mexico, fashioning with records of 18-3, and a 1.82 ERA for Tampico and in 1939, 16-6 with a 2.50 ERA. This included stints of 40 scoreless innings, and two no-hitters. Chet was credited with a 127-79 NL record, a 62% winning percentage.

Chet Brewer had a wide range of experiences. In 1934, he pitched against an all-star team, which included Jimmie Foxx and Heinie Manush (HOFers). Then, he was the manager of the Kansas City Royal who were playing in a winter league that featured Bob Feller (a HOFer), and other major leaguers from the status quo league. Chet should have already been in the HOF.

4.) Dixon, Herbert Albert (Rap)

Active From: 1922-37 Positions: **RF,** CF, LF, 3B, P, Manager
Teams: Harrisburg Giants, Washington Potomacs, Chicago American Giants, Baltimore Black Sox, Hilldale Daises, Pittsburgh Crawfords, Washington Pilots, Philadelphia Stars, Brooklyn Eagles, New York Cubans, and the Homestead Grays.

As an outstanding outfielder who played with some great teams, Rap had great speed and range. He was also a great defensive player. He was a tremendous power hitter and was one of the best hitters in the beginning of the organized Negro Leagues (20's and 30's).

Those great teams he played for included the 1929 American Negro League Champions, the Baltimore Black Sox, and the Pittsburgh Crawfords of the mid-30's. For the '29 team, (Black Sox) he hit .432 with 16 homeruns, had 25 stolen bases, and a .784 slugging percentage. In 1932, for Gus Greenlee's Crawfords he had a .357 B. A., and had 15 homeruns.

In 1924, his Harrisburg team joined the Eastern Colored League. He hit cleanup in the lineup behind Oscar Charleston (HOFer). The next two years (1925-26), he hit .357 and .358 respectively.

Dixon was considered an intelligent player who hit for average and power. He finished his Negro League career with a .340 B. A., and a 362 B. A. against the status quo.

Dixon played in the NL for 16 years, and was honored in 1933 by being selected to join the first ever East-West all-star game played in the NL…he belongs.

5.) Donaldson, John Wesley

Active From: 1913-34 Positions: **P**, OF
Teams: All Nations, Gilkerson's Union Giants, Chicago Giants, Indianapolis ABCs, Brooklyn Royal Giants, Lincoln Giants, Detroit Stars, and the Kansas City Monarchs.

John Donaldson was a great curveball pitcher. He had an assortment of curves, a good fastball, and a great changeup. He was one of the best lefthanders in Black baseball. At times during his career, the southpaw was unhittable.

John did some barnstorming earlier in his career in the Midwest. Once, while playing for a team in Minnesota in 1913, he pitched a 12 inning one-hitter, and struck out 27. In 1915 at Sioux Falls, he fanned 35 batters in an 18-inning game losing 1-0.

The first of the best times for him was in the 10's when he played for J. L. Wilkinson's multi-racial All-Nations team from 1913 to 1917. Donaldson averaged 20 strikeouts per game with that team, and pitched three consecutive no-hitters. In 1915, at one point he had 92 strikeouts in 56 innings pitched. He continued that hot streak to 252 strikeouts in 15 games. The next year he had 240 strikeouts in 12 games.

When the NL organized in 1920, J. L. Wilikinson sought after and reunited with Donaldson. Wilkinson said that Donaldson was "the most amazing pitcher he had ever seen."

John's career spanned four decades…From barnstorming with the Tennessee Rats in 1912 to his final full season with the Monarchs in 1934. In 1945, he played some with the Monarch's traveling club. NL authorities have put him in the class with the greatest Black lefthanders like Nip Winters, Willie Foster, and Slim Jones. They are considered the best southpaws in Black baseball, and only Willie Foster has been placed in the HOF.

<u>COMPLIMENTS ON DONALDSON</u>

1.) John Henry Lloyd (HOFer)— "The toughest pitcher I've ever faced."
2.) John McGraw, then Manager of the New York Giants— "Donaldson would be worth $50,000 if he were White."
3.) A New York State League manager offered him $10,000 to pass as a Cuban and pitch on his team.

"No longer to struggle with respect and rejection,
Other countries welcomed you, and you received real affection."

Finally, Donaldson created his own team, the John Donaldson all-stars '31-'32. When the color line was lifted, he became a scout for the Chicago White Sox. The **Hall** would be a better place with him.

6.) <u>Hill, J. Preston (Pete)</u>
Active From: 1899-1926 Positions: **<u>CF, LF</u>**, RF, 2B, Manager, Business Manager
Teams: Pittsburgh Keystones, Cuban X-Giants, Philadelphia Giants, Leland Giants, Chicago American Giants, Detroit Stars, Milwaukee Bears, and the Baltimore Black Sox.

Pete was a great and marvelous hitter who hit for average and power. Hill used the completed field, excelled in bunting, and had great speed. He seldom struck out, and was one of the fastest outfielders in the game. He was a flawless fielder, and had a deadly arm. Sounds a little like Willie Mays to me. As a base stealer, he's compared to Jackie Robinson.

In 1911, he hit safely in 115 of 116 games. Some experts compared him to Ty Cobb. In fact, in the era he played, it is said that Tris Speaker and Ty Cobb would flank Hill for the best outfield.

In 1903, he signed with the newly organized Philadelphia Giants. There he joined with Rube Foster. They won consecutive championships in 1905 and 1906.

When Foster moved to the Leland Giants, Hill went with him. In 1910 when Foster split with Leland, Pete left again to join Foster. This team finished with a 106-7 record and Pete was a big part of it. Authorities say that if an MVP were selected that year, it would have been Hill.

Foster claimed that this 1910 team was "the greatest team Black or White of "all time." Hill was the team captain and hit .428…outhitting teammate HOFer John Henry Lloyd.

Hill posted these averages; in 1911 (the year of the streak) .400, 1912 .357, and 1914 .302. Pete was sometimes allowed to manage the team, and in 1919 became playing manager of the Detroit Stars.

Ben Taylor made this statement about Pete Hill at the twilight of his career. "The time was he was numbered among the greatest in the game, and he will probably never have an equal as a hitter. I think he is the most dangerous man in a pinch in baseball." Hill played for 27 year in the NL. He closed out his great career with a lifetime .326 B. A. in the NL, and a .354 lifetime B. A. against the status quo.

Finally, in 1944 Cum Posey selected Hill to his all-time all-star team calling Hill "the most consistent hitter of my lifetime."

7.) <u>Jenkins, Clarence (Fats)</u>

Active From: 1920-40 Positions: <u>**OF,**</u> Manager

Teams: New York Lincoln Giants, Atlantic City Bacharach Giants, Harrisburg Giants, Hilldale Daises, Baltimore Black Sox, New York Harlem Stars, Pittsburgh Crawfords, New York Black Yankees, Brooklyn Eagles, Brooklyn Royal Giants, Toledo Crawfords, and the Philadelphia Stars.

At 5' 7" and 180 pounds, Fats was exceptional fast. He threw and hit from the left side. He didn't have much power, but he was a spray hitter. A kind of shorter virgin of Tony Gwynn. Like Gwynn, Jenkins was a very versatile and talented athlete. He played basketball with the famous Renaissance basketball team during the off-seasons.

He started his professional baseball career in 1920 with the powerful New York Lincoln Giants…the first year the NL was organized. Fats always maintained a high batting average and was an excellent leadoff man.

In 1931, he played with HOFer John Henry Lloyd's New York Harlem Stars. He appeared in several East-West All—Star games including the first one in 1933. Fats played in the Negro Leagues for 21 years, and accumulated a .334 lifetime B. A.

Fats spent most of his 21 years with the New York teams (Giants & Yankees). I don't know of a player today who hits .334 for 21 years and is not in the HOF. During a ten year span 1932-42, Jenkins was the captain of the New York Black Yankees. He led the team to an 88 game winning streak during the 1934 & '35 seasons. He was an early Deion Sanders.

8.) **Johnson, Grant (Homerun)**
Active From: 1895-1916 Positions: **SS**, 2B, P, Manager
Teams: Page Fence Giants, Chicago Columbia Giants, Chicago Union, Cuban X-Giants, Philadelphia Giants, Brooklyn Royal Giants, Leland Giants, Chicago Giants, New York Giants, Mohawk Giants, and the New York Lincoln Stars.

Homerun Johnson (as he was applicable called) was the most famous homerun hitter in the dead-ball era before John Henry Lloyd.

Before joining the Cuban X-Giants, the Philadelphia Giants, and others including the Leland Giants and HOFer Rube Foster, Johnson and Bud Fowler formed the Page Fence Giants in 1895-98. Johnson was the captain and shortstop. In 1895, he batted .471, and the team's record was 118-36.

For the great 1910 Leland's team, Johnson hit .397 in the third slot. He followed this with a B. A. of 374, .413, and .371 from 1911 to 1913 with the powerful New York Lincoln Giants.

Johnson spent some quality time in that "far away land" in Cuba. He captained the Havana Reds to the winter league championship, and became the first American to win a batting title. His five-year average was .319.

The game of interest that everyone talked about was the game between the Havana team and the Detroit Tigers (my spring training home team). Johnson out hit Ty Cobb, and Sam Crawford in the 1910 series.

In the seasons with the New York Lincoln Giants, Johnson batted cleanup behind John Henry Lloyd. They won the eastern title and beat Rube Foster and the Chicago American Giants.

In the games against the status quo Johnson's B. A. was .293. My calculations say Johnson had a .368 B. A. in the Negro Leagues. He played for 22 years. Cooperstown should've had him set up.

9.) <u>Lundy, Richard (Dick, King Richard)</u>
Active From: 1916-39 Positions: <u>SS</u>, 3B, 2B, C, Manager
Teams: Atlantic City Bacharach Giants, Havana Reds, Daisies, New York Lincoln Giants, Baltimore Black Sox, Philadelphia Stars, Newark Dodgers, New York Cubans, Newark Eagles, Atlanta Black Crackers, and the Brooklyn Royal Giants.

Lundy (my fellow alumnus) has been called the best shortstop in Black or White baseball during the 1920's. A switch hitter who hit for average and big power, he followed Lloyd and preceded Wells (HOF inductees). Defensively, he had a wide range has a SS, and a very strong arm. All of this and being very graceful allowed him to play a deep shortstop.

I like the fact that we attended the same college, Florida Baptist Academy in St. Augustine, Florida, which is now Florida Memorial College currently in Miami, Florida. You learn these things in freshman orientation.

In 1920, King Richard was so much in demand and so popular, he was taken to court because he had signed contracts with three clubs…at the same time. The court ruled that he had to return to the Bacharach's team.

When John Henry Lloyd came to the team in 1924 as a player-manager, he did not hesitate to place Dick at SS, and himself at 2nd base, because he recognized that Dick's ability at SS was far superior to his. For the years 1921-29, his batting averages were .484, .335, .310, .363, .273, .347, .341, .409, and .336.

Lundy was respected by all of his teammates, and served as captain from 1923-25. In 1926-1928, he served as playing manager. He directed them to win the championship of the Eastern Colored League (at that time), but lost in the "World Series" to the Chicago American Giants. Lundy hit .325, and stole 6 bases in the first series, and .250 in the second series.

In 1929, King Richard was traded to the Baltimore Black Sox for Ben Taylor, Mac Eggleston, and cash. Because the managers were exchanged, Lundy guided the Black Sox to the American Negro League pennant. Lundy had a 336 B. A. and had 16 stolen bases despite being injured. The Sox infield that year featured Lundy, Marcelle, and Frank Warfield. They were called the *"million dollar infield."*

<u>Complimentary</u> statements <u>by</u> two <u>Hall</u> of <u>Famers</u>
   (1.) "I wish I could paint that Lundy White" —John McGraw, New York Giants manager.
   (2.) "The greatest shortstop to ever live." —Honus Wagner, Hall of Famer.

King Richard's lifetime B. A. in the Negro League was .330. His lifetime average against the status quo was .344. The **King** belongs.

10.)<u>Mackey, Raleigh (Biz)</u>

Active From: 1920-1947 Positions: <u>C,</u> SS, 3B, 2B, 1B, OF, P, Manager
Teams: Indianapolis ABCs, New York Lincoln Giants, Colored all-stars, Hilldale Daisies, Philadelphia Royal Giants, Washington Elite Giants, Philadelphia Stars, Newark Dodgers, and the Newark Eagles.

Someone said, to see Biz Mackey play is to see Roy Campanella play. Well, I certainly saw a lot of Roy, and I think he was the greatest catcher in my lifetime. Of course, I maybe a little partial because of my connection with the Dodger Blue. However, when I read about the things Biz did, I knew he needed to be in the HOF…now.

The first word I used to describe Roy was cool. That was the description I first saw when I looked up Mackey, "cool under pressure." Mackey was considered to be a master at defense and calming to pitchers. He could snap throws to second in a squatting position just like Campanella. He was intelligent and had good baseball sense. He depended on observation and memory.

Because of his agility, he was able to play other positions. Biz was a dangerous switch-hitter with great power.

In Hilldale's first season, Mackey had a B. A. of .423, 20 homeruns, and a .698 slugging percentage for his team in the Eastern Colored League in 1923. From 1924-31, his averages remain constant at .337, .350, .327, .315, .327, .337, .400, and .376.

He led the Hilldale team to three consecutive pennants and a "World Series" in 1925. In that series, Mackey batted .375. When Mackey started with the ABCs under C. I. Taylor, he learned from a master teacher. In three seasons there, he had batting averages of .308, .296, and .391 respectively.

Once the Eastern Colored League was organized in 1923, the Negro National League got raided, and Hilldale's Ed Bolden, the team's owner, selected Mackey.

Biz was very popular for NL teams in exhibition games against the status quo. In 1926 Hilldale played the Philadelphia Athletics featuring HOFer Lefty Grove and won 5 out 6 games. Then playing with the Philadelphia Royal Giants in 1921 and 1922, Biz hit a combined .382 B. A. against a team headed up by Bob Meusel and his brother Irish. The NL stars won 7 out of 11 games.

When Mackey toured the Orient in 1934-35, he was very popular with the Japanese people. The Japanese people seem to enjoy the shadow ball exhibitions.

In 1933, Biz was selected for the East-West all-star game over a youngster by the name of Josh Gibson. Gibson was just starting out, and Mackey was the veteran.

Although Mackey has been given credit for the tutelage of several young players like Campanella, Irvin, Doby, and Newcombe, he was still a great player in his own right, and should be in the HOF on his own merits.

His lifetime average in the NL for 28 years is .335, and against the status quo in exhibition games it is .326.

11.)Mendez, Jose` (Joe, The Black Diamond-a.k.a. Jose` Mendez Baez)
Active From: 1908-1926 Positions: **P**, SS, 3B, 2B, OF, Manager
Teams: Brooklyn Royal Giants, Cuban Stars, Stars of Cuba, All Nations, Chicago American Giants, Detroit Stars, and the Kansas City Monarchs.

(Additional information is already mentioned in Chapter III)

Jose` Mendez was nicknamed the Black Diamond. He was one of the greatest pitchers to grace the diamond in the early twentieth century. Mendez also played other positions, and he was a fair hitter, but he had few pitchers in his class.

This Cuban was smooth, wiry, fast, and deceptive. The pitcher I would compare him today with is Pedro Martinez. He had long arms and was exceptional fast. Many experts say he was faster than Smokey Joe Williams. He started in Cuba in 1903 at the age of sixteen. He started in the NL in 1908 with the Brooklyn Royal Giants posting a 3-0 ledger. In 1909, he moved onto the Cuban Stars and posted a record of 44-2.

Mendez defeated HOFers Christy Mathewson, and Eddie Plank in exhibition games in Cuba. In 1912, again he defeated Christy Mathewson (4-3 in 10 innings), and Nap Rucker (2-1) all within three days.

After those exhibitions, John McGraw (of the "World Champion" New York Giants) said that Mendez was a "sort of Walter Johnson and Grover Alexander rolled into one." He said that if he were White, he would be worth $30,000 a year. He also said he would welcome him (if he were allowed) on the Giants teams.

After developing arm trouble and taking occasional turns on the mound with several teams, he begin to return to form when he rejoined J. L. Wilkinson, but this time with the Kansas City Monarchs. They were joining the Negro National League as a new team in 1920. He was the playing manager who played shortstop and pitched occasionally.

Jose` led the Monarchs to pennants in 1923, '24, and '25. Here Mendez reinvented himself and brought back the Mendez of old. He led the Monarchs into the "World Series" against the champions of the Eastern Colored League, the Hilldale Daisies.

John Henry Lloyd (a HOFer) who faced most of the great pitchers of that time said, he never saw a pitcher better than Mendez. That is a great statement, and I believe an endorsement for the HOF coming from John Henry Lloyd.

In 1939, the first class of HOFers was inducted into the Cuban Hall of Fame, Mendez was in that class.

12.) Monroe, William (Bill)
Active From: 1896-1914 Positions: **2B, 3b, SS,** IB
Teams: Chicago Unions, Cuban X-Giants, Philadelphia Giants, Brooklyn Royal Giants, Quaker Giants of New York, Chicago American Giants, and the Chicago Giants.

One of the first real great Black players in the deadball era, and before the NL organized in 1920.

Monroe was a crowd-pleaser; he was a highly skilled infielder who entertained the fans with showmanship while demonstrating accuracy. Here is an example of showmanship by Monroe, and at the same time prove how great a player he really was.

Hall of Famer Joe McGinnity was pitching for a team against Monroe, and his Philadelphia Giants team. McGinnity was paid $500 to pitch the game, and Monroe got him to bet all of it that he would best him in the game.

When Monroe came to the plate after 7 innings, the score was still tied. Monroe pointed to the bat (intimidating) toward McGinnity, and McGinnity took exception to it. He knocked down Monroe on the next pitch. Monroe got up and repeated the act. McGinnity knocked him down a second time.

They exchanged words until Monroe said, "I'll bet you $500 that I'll hit a homerun." McGinnity said, "it's a bet." McGinnity fired his fastball on the next pitch, and Monroe hit a homerun that was the winning run.

The showmanship came when Monroe decided to run the bases backwards. This would get on McGinnity's nerves, and it would be what the fans came to see.

Monroe helped Philadelphia win three championships from 1904 to 1906, while playing three different positions—shortstop, third base, and second base consecutively.

He joined Rube Foster in 1911, and hit in the cleanup spot behind Pete Hill. By 1914, Rube Foster had assembled another great team together by bring aboard John Henry Lloyd. Monroe hit .348, and was dubbed "king of second baseman." Monroe passed away the next year.

Sol White, Rube Foster, and Dan McCleland and had very high praise for Monroe. John McGraw said that Monroe was the greatest player of all time, and would have been a star (not just a great player) in the status quo major leagues, but he was denied "chance and opportunity."

It was rumored that McGraw wanted to pass Monroe off as a Cuban so he could play for him, and the New York Giants.

13.) Oms, Alejandro (El Caballero, Walla Walla, Papa)
Active From: 1917-35 Positions: **CF,** LF, RF, P
Teams: Cubans Stars (East), All Cubans, and the New York Cubans.

Alejandro Oms was the center fielder for the great, great outfield of the Cuban Stars in the Eastern Colored League. Bernardo Baro, and Pablo Mesa, two great players in their own right flanked him in the outfield.

Oms had a wide range, and a strong accurate arm. A very fast runner, a great base stealer, Oms was best known for his bat.

He was a lefty, and hit to all fields with power. Oms was the first one to hit 40 homeruns in the early 20's. During the 6 years he played in the Eastern Colored League, he was paired (hitting third and fourth) with HOFer Martin Dihigo. He had a .340 batting average during that time; recording averages of .400, .326, .318, .342, .348, and .308.

In 1935, Oms batted clean-up and hit, .381 to help the New York Cubans win the second-half pennant. They lost to the Pittsburgh Crawfords in the championship game.

In 1935, Oms ended his 18 NL career, but he was not finished as a player. During the 40's, he played in Venezuela, and was a great player there. Earlier in his career, he played for 15 years in Cuba and had a lifetime .351 B. A. In his 18 years in the NL, he finished with a .332 B. A.

Oms set the record for hitting over .300 for 11 consecutive times. A proven winner, Oms played for four championship teams. He was elected to the Cuban HOF in 1944. The player Oms is compared to is HOFer Paul Waner.

14.)PETWAY, BRUCE (BUDDY)
> Active From: 1906-25 Positions: **C,** IB, OF, Manager
> Teams: Cuban X-Giants, Leland Giants, Brooklyn Royal Giants, Philadelphia Giants, Chicago American Giants, and the Detroit Stars.

Many experts feel that Petway was one of the greatest catchers of his lifetime, and of all time. He had a strong and accurate arm, and he often threw out runners from his knees.

In 1910 in an exhibition game in Cuba, the Havana Reds were playing the Detroit Tigers once again. The Reds had beaten them before.

Bruce Petway and John Henry Lloyd of HOF talents led the Reds. Ty Cobb (also of HOF talents) attempted to steal second base three times; and three times Petway threw him out. Rumor had it that after Cobb had been thrown out for the third time, he ran off the field cursing, and swearing never to play against Blacks again. Petway hit .390 against the Tigers.

Bruce Petway was the first great Black catcher. Not only that, but he was studying to become a medical doctor when he abandon his studies to join the ranks of professional baseball.

In 1910 for the regular season, he joined John Henry Lloyd, Frank Duncan, and Rube Foster's Leland Giants for "the greatest team of all time." Petway hit

.393 for that team. Also unusual for a catcher, he was a very good base stealer, great bunter, and was often used for a leadoff man. He most certainly belongs.

15.) Poles, Spottswood (Spot)
Active From: 1909-23 Position: **CF**
Teams: Philadelphia Giants, New York Lincoln Giants, Brooklyn Royal Giants, New York Lincoln Stars, Hilldale Daisies, New York Bacharach Giants, and the Richmond Giants.

Spot was a switch hitting center fielder with great speed. For some reason, he was labeled the "Black Ty Cobb." Spot's speed has been compared to Cool Papa Bell's.

Professional, Poles started his career with Sol White at Philadelphia. He played there for two years, and then followed Sol to the New York Lincoln Giants. That year, (1911) Spot stole 41 bases in 60 games. His statistics for the first four years were. .440, .398, .414, and .487.

In a game in 1913 against HOFer Grover Cleveland Alexander, Spot had three straight hits. This was one of Sol White's team who handily defeating one of Rube Foster's great teams…the Chicago American Giants in the championship play-offs.

In 1918, Spot enter the army during World War I, and was as outstanding in battle as he was on the baseball diamond. He earned five stars, and a Purple Heart. This was the same time my great uncle, Thomas Hightower was serving.

When Poles returned, he played with four different teams. The Lincoln Giants, Hilldale Daisies, Bacharachs (Atlantic City), and back again to the Giants.

After 15 years, he retired with a .400 B. A. in the Negro Leagues, and ended up with a .594 B. A. against the status quo.

John McGraw made the final stamp on Spot. McGraw, then the manager of the New York Giants said that Poles would be one of the four Black players he would want if the "color line" were lifted.

Poles and his wife are buried in Arlington National Cemetery. After a lifetime batting average of .400 for 15 years, if Poles is not a HOFer, who is?

16.) Redding, Richard (Cannonball Dick)
From: 1911-38 Positions: **P**, OF, Manager
Teams: Philadelphia Giants, New York Lincoln Giants, New York Lincoln Stars, Indianapolis ABCs, Brooklyn Royal Giants, Chicago American Giants, Atlantic City Bacharachs, and the New York Bacharachs.

Cannonball Dick Redding, one of the truly great pitchers, before and into the organization of the NL in 1920. He was another player coveted by John McGraw of the New York Giants for his team if the "color line" were dropped.

The tall over powering right-hander was amongst the top Black pitchers, and pitchers in general in the 10's. Dick Redding used a no wind-up delivery long before Don Larsen made it famous in the 1956 "World Series."

Redding was credited with a total of 30 no hitters against all competition levels. As a rookie in 1911, he won 17 straight games with just speed and control. The following year, 1912, he was teamed up with the great Smokey Joe Williams and had a ledger of 43-12. He had several no-hitters that year, and in one game he actually struck out 25 of the maximum 27 batters he faced.

After a few other stops, Redding joined Rube Foster's Chicago American Giants and went 33-3. This was the year; he was compared to Walter Johnson. Redding was a great and gifted NL's player, and his credentials leave no doubts to me.

17.) Rogan, Wilbur (Bullet) a.k.a. Bullet Joe
    From: 1917-46 Positions: **P, OF,** IB, 2B, 3B, SS, Manager, Umpire
    Teams: Kansas City Colored Giants, All Nations, and the Kansas City Monarchs.

This tough Buffalo soldier was discovered by Casey Stengel one day while pitching for the United Stated cavalry. Casey reported the information to J. L. Wilkinson, then owner of the All Nation's team.

Joe was a Babe Ruth type player in that he was not just a great pitcher, but a great hitter, and fielder in the outfield as well at 2nd and 3rd bases.

Joe hit .400 in the Negro Leagues, and .389 versus the status quo leagues. He was replaced by Satchel Paige as the ace of the Kansas City Monarchs. Dizzy Dean called him a showboat and said, "he never gave you a good ball to hit. He should be in the HOF." Some NL stars agree that Rogan was a better pitcher than Satchel. His record as a pitcher was 113-45, a .715 percentage. What was interesting however, was that Bullet Joe led the league in wins as a pitcher, while he was hitting in the clean-up spot as one of the league's top hitters.

Finally, at the age of 48 in a game against Bob Feller's All-Stars, Rogan had 3 hits.
    ***Bullet was inducted into the HOF in 1998.**

18.) <u>Santop, Louis (Top, Big Bertha) a.k.a. Louis Santop Loftin</u> (his name)
From: 1909-1926 Positions: <u>C</u>, IB, LF, 3B, Manager
Teams: Philadelphia Giants, New York Lincoln Giants, Brooklyn Royal Giants, Chicago American Giants, New York Lincoln Stars, and the Hilldale Daisies.

A big man at 6feet 4inches and 240 pounds. He was a great catcher. He was a great homerun hitter, and was known for monster clouts over 500 feet.

Top, as he was affectionately called could throw a ball from home plate to over the centerfield wall. The big Texan used a big heavy bat in the dead ball era.

A left-handed hitter, Top had a lifetime .406 B. A. in the Negro Leagues, and a .316 lifetime B. A. against the status quo.

Earlier in his career, Santop was paid $500 a month, and he was another great Black baseball player always compared to Babe Ruth. Torriente and Gibson were two others. Top was probably compared to Ruth because he used to call his homerun shots, and because of his consistency, and his great power.

In a 1920 post-season game against Casey Stengel's all-stars Top had 3 hits, while the Babe went hitless and struck out two times.

The famous 1932 post-season "World Series" homerun call by Ruth was often done by Top.

One time while playing a game in Atlantic City, a lady fan yelled at him when he was on deck. She told Top that he was going to strikeout when he came to the plate. Top looked at her, shook his head and pointed to the right-field fence. The women yelled, "I bet you a buck?"

Top got a dollar from the dugout, and stuck it in the screen at the grandstand. He was the next batter and he put the ball far over the right-field fence.

Top missed the 1918 & 1919 seasons because of World War I. After the war, he returned to Ed Bolden's Hilldale team and spent the remainder of his playing career with them including pennant-winning teams from 1924-25.

As Black baseball's first legitimate homerun hitter and one of Black baseball's first great catchers, many Negro League vets say Santop belongs in the HOF.

19.) <u>Smith, Hilton Lee</u>
From: 1932-48 Positions: <u>P</u>, OF, IB
Teams: Monroe Monarchs, New Orleans Black Creoles, New Orleans Crescent Stars, Kansas City Monarchs.

Hilton Smith was probably most famously known for being Satchel's relief pitcher, but he was much more than that. This was toward the end of Satchel's career, at least in the Negro Leagues, and Smith would actually pitch the majority of the games started by Satchel.

A lot of historians and Bob Feller believed that Smith was better than Paige. After seeing Smith pitch in the fall of 1941, Feller concluded that Smith was better.

It was believed that Smith possessed the best curve in the game. He did not gain popularity and receive recognition, because he was quiet and stayed in the background.

Some experts also believed that the right-hander's pitching repertoire with his great curve ball, rising fastball, sinker, slider, and great changeup were the best at his time.

Smith pitched in six consecutive all-star games, tying Satchel Paige for second place on the all-time NL all-star list. His great all-star years coincided with the years the Monarchs were champions of the Negro Major Leagues. Smith's lifetime pitching record is 161-32 in league play, an 83% winning record. Anyone in the HOF with better credentials? (Silence) I didn't think so.

20.) **Stearns, Norman Thomas (Turkey)**
From: 1923-42 Positions: **CF**, IF, IB
Teams: Detroit Stars, New York Lincoln Giants, Kansas City Monarchs, Cole's American Giants, Philadelphia Stars, Chicago American Giants, Detroit Black Sox, and the Toledo Cubs.

Another should have been HOFer is Norman "Turkey" Stearns. A small man in stature at just under 170 pounds, you would not believe the bat speed he created for a small man.

Many believed that he was the greatest lead off man of all-time in any league, including Ty Cobb.

In 1932, Stearns led the league in doubles, triples, homeruns, and steals. No status player to my knowledge has ever done that. He was sought of a Rickey Henderson with more power.

He had an uncanny batting stance. A left-handed power hitter who turned his right toes vertical to the ground. In 1923, '24, and '25, he led the league in homeruns, and he did this four other times.

In nine years (1923-31) with Detroit alone, this is what he hit; .365, .358, .369, .375, .346, .326, .378, .340, and .350. In none of these years did he hit his highest B. A. In 1935, he hit a league high .430.

Stearns ended his 20-year career with 185 league homeruns, 7 homerun titles, and a .359 B. A. in the Negro Leagues, and a .351 B. A. in exhibition games against the status quo. There are no HOF doubts here.

21.)Suttles, George (Mule)
From: 1923-44 Positions: **IB, LF**, RF, Manager, umpire
Teams: Birmingham Black Barons, St. Louis Stars, Baltimore Black Sox, Detroit Wolves, Washington Pilots, Cole's American Giants, Newark Eagles, Indianapolis ABCs, and the New York Black Yankees.

The 6 foot 3 inch 215 pound coal-miner was a powerful hitter who maintained a good average and used a 50-ounce bat. He was as powerful a hitter as anyone in the NL. Reportedly, Mule is the all-time champion for homeruns in the Negro Leagues.

Most of Mule Suttles' teammates have attested to his tremendous and unusual power. Willie Wells, Leon Day, and Ray Dandrige all have told stories about Mule's abilities to hit balls 500, and even 600 feet.

In 1926, Suttles was with the St. Louis Stars, and these are his statistics; 26 homeruns, .432 B. A., and a 1.000 slugging percentage. In 1930, with the same team he hit .384, and had a .837 slugging percentage. Suttles constantly hit homeruns on an average of one every 10 at bats.

In 1936, Suttles joined the Newark Eagles and part of the soon to be "million-dollar-infield." These are the statistics for the first four years:

1936—36 Homeruns, .396 B. A.,
1937—36   "   .356   "
1938—26   "   .420   "
1939—   .325   "

Suttles played in five all-stars games and produced a .412 B. A., and an .883 slugging percentage. He was highly sought after for barnstorming tours. In an exhibition game against the Chicago Cubs, Jim Weaver was the pitcher. Suttles had singled, doubled, and tripled before coming to the bat to complete the cycle. Weaver asked shortstop Leo Durocher how he thought Suttles should be pitched to? Durocher told him to "just pitch and pray."

Suttles is credited with a .374 lifetime batting average against the status quo, and for his 22 years in the Negro Leagues a .338 batting average.

22.)Taylor, Benjamin H. (Ben)
From: 1910-40 Positions: **IB**, P., Manager, Umpire.
Teams: West Baden Sprudels, St. Louis Giants, New York Lincoln Giants, Indianapolis ABCs, Hilldale Daisies, New York Bacharach Giants, Washington Potomacs, Harrisburg Giants, Baltimore Black Sox, Atlantic City Bacharach Giants, California Stars, Silver Moons, Washington Pilots, Baltimore Stars, Brooklyn Eagles, Washington Black Senators, Washington Royals, and the New York Cubans.

Considered to be the premier first baseman before the time of Buck Leonard. Ben Taylor is from a family of baseball players. Taylor played with a few teams early on, but did not really become great until he came to the Indianapolis ABC's and teamed up with his brother, C. I. Taylor in 1914. He started and stayed in the clean-up spot throughout his tenure for the ABC's.

The left-handed hitter was one of the most productive in the dead-ball era. He maintained a lifetime batting average of .334 in the NL. Ben hit over .300 in 15 of the 16 years he played in the Negro Leagues.

Between 1918 and 1920, Ben was back and forth between the Bacharch Giants and the ABC's. From 1920 to 1922 with the ABC's Ben hit .323, .407, and .358. In 1924, he hit .314, and had 15 homeruns. After teaming up with Oscar Charleston in 1925 at Harrisburg, he hit .328 as playing manager. At age 41 with the Giants, he hit .322.

Ben Taylor finished his NL career having tutored many greats, some in the HOF. He also is deserving of a place for himself in the HOF.

23.) <u>Thomas, Clinton Cyrus (Clint, Hawk)</u>
From: 1920-38 Positions: **CF**, RF, 2B.
Teams: Brooklyn Royal Giants, Columbus Buckeyes, Detroit Stars, Hilldale Daisies, Atlantic City Bacharach Giants, New York Lincoln Giants, New York Harlem Stars, Indianapolis ABCs, New York Black Yankees, Newark Eagles, and the Philadelphia Stars.

Dubbed "Hawk" by Detroit Stars Manager Bruce Petway, this ball hawking center fielder was blessed with speed, power, and a good bat. After such continuous demonstrations, he was moved from 2nd base to right field.

Thomas started his professional career just as professional baseball for African-Americans was organized in 1920. After being seen in a tryout by John Henry Lloyd (HOFer), then manager of the Brooklyn Royal Giants, he was signed.

The next year, Lloyd moved on to manage the Columbus Buckeyes, and he took Hawk with him. Thomas responded with a .281 batting average. In 1922, with a new team the Detroit Stars, he hit .342.

In 1926-27 for Hilldale he hit .306, and .279. When the Eastern Colored League broke up; he joined the Bacharach Giants, and continued to be impressive with a .342 B. A.

Early in Thomas' career, he played winter ball in Cuba, where he was exposed to Aldolfo Luque (mentioned in Chapter III). He responded with a six-year total of .310.

Thomas was known for having great games against the status quo. In 1934 against the status quo champs and Dizzy Dean in an exhibition game with the score tied at 0-0, Hawk came to bat in the ninth inning and hit a triple, then stole home to win the game 1-0.

Because he played in Yankee Stadium with the Black Yankees, Thomas was often called the "Black Joe DiMaggio." In his last season, Hawk hit .342. Thomas completed his 19-year career with a .300 batting average, and 367 homeruns.

24.) Torriente, Cristobal (a.k.a.) Cristobel (Carlos) Torriente
   From: 1913-1928 Positions: **CF**, LF, RF, P, 3B, IB.
   Teams: Cuban Stars, All Nations, Chicago American Giants, Kansas City Monarchs, and the Detroit Stars.

Cristobal Torriente a "dark Cuban" super star, and very much deserving of the HOF was playing in a game against Babe Ruth in Cuba in 1920. Torriente hit 3 homeruns and a double. An American newspaper called him "the Babe Ruth of Cuba." Why not call Babe Ruth the Cristobal Torriente of America?" Beginning with giving some honor to Babe Ruth, I don't think that the last time I saw the words "super star" he had exclusive rights...even in baseball.

Of course I know that he was wrongfully given those rights by the status quo press. This is another example of the lack of respect shown to NL players like Cristobal. This was 1920, not 1913 when Cristobal was a rookie. He was already an established star in his own rights beginning with the Chicago American Giants in 1918.

Cristobal was with Chicago at the beginning of the organization of the Negro National Leagues. These are his statistics for the first four years: .411, .338, .342, and .412. He won the batting titles in 1920, and 1923. He was traded to the K. C. Monarchs in 1926 and led the team to the first half champion with a .407 batting average.

Cristobal finished up in the Negro Leagues with the Detroit Stars in 1927-28, .339, and .320. He had several stints with some minor teams after he got older.

Hall of Fame umpire, Jocko Conlan thought that Torriente was a great hitter who belonged in the HOF. The New York Giants sought after him and wanted to sign him because he was a Cuban, but after an examination of his hair, they decided against it.

Torriente hit .333 lifetime in the NL, and .313 against the status quo.

25.) Williams, Joseph (Joe, Smokey Joe, Cyclone, Yank)
   From: 1910-32 Positions: **P**, OF, IB, Manager
   Teams: Chicago Giants, New York Lincoln Giants, Mohawk Giants, Chicago American Giants, Atlantic City Bacharach Giants, Hilldale Daisies, Brooklyn Royal Giants, Homestead Grays, and the Detroit Wolves.

I could justify Smokey Joe's HOF credentials by this HOFers' statement.

"Had he been able to pitch in the (status quo) major leagues, he would have been a yearly 30 game winner." —Ty Cobb.

All the more reason that the Negro League stars of the past would have been/could have been stars in the status quo league just as they are today.

Smokey Joe was once voted the greatest Negro League pitcher of all time over Satchel Paige. He has beaten face to face such HOFers as Walter Johnson, Grover Cleveland Alexander, Chief Bender, Rube Marquard, Waite Hoyt, and others.

Smokey Joe would on several occasions strike out 20 or more batters. In post season play in 1912, he shutout the "World Champion" New York Giants 6-0.

In 1915, he struck out 10 batters throwing a 3-hit shutout at Grover Cleveland Alexander and the Philadelphia Phillies.

In 1917, Smokey threw a no-hitter at the New York Giants and struck out 20 batters, but he lost the game 1-0 on an error. Smokey Joe Williams beat the Giants twice before in a 3-game series. People who saw both Satchel and Smokey Joe swear that Smokey was Satchel's equal, or could have been better.

1914 was Smokey's best year in that his record was 41 and 3 against the Negro Leagues and the status quo leagues. His record against the status quo is 21-7 lifetime.

*Smokey Joe Williams was named in 1999 to the Major League Baseball Hall Of Fame.

26.) Wilson, Ernest Judson (Jud, Boojum)
From: 1922-45 Positions: **3B, IB,** 2B, SS, OF, MAN.
Teams: Baltimore Black Sox, Homestead Grays, Pittsburgh Crawfords, and the Philadelphia Stars.

Satchel Paige said, he was "one of the two best hitters in Black baseball." That alone was enough for me to check out Mr. "Boojum Wilson," better known as Jud. What I found out was that Jud was a HOF player, and somewhat of a character. He got into and out of trouble with umpires, and players.

Cum Posey considered him to be the most dangerous and consistent hitter in Black baseball. Cum placed Jud on the all-time All-American team for a national magazine in 1945.

In 1923, his second season with the Black Sox, he won the batting title hitting .373. These are his averages through 1937—.377, .395, .346, .468, .376, .350, .372, .323, .356, .354, .342, .324, .315, and .386.

Jud played in Cuba for 6 winter seasons with a lifetime B. A. there of .372. He won the batting title there twice; once in 1925 with a .403 B. A., and again in 1926 at .441.

This powerful left-handed hitter finished a lifetime B, A. in the Negro Leagues hitting .345, and a lifetime B. A. against the status quo at .442.

During a 6-year period from 1929 to 1934, he played with 4 championship teams. The 1929 Baltimore Black Sox, the 1931 Homestead Grays, (believed by some to be the greatest Black team of all-time) and a team Jud captained, the 1932 Pittsburgh Crawfords, another great team (my choice for the greatest team of all time), and the 1934 Philadelphia Stars.

Jud hit .522 the first half of his rookie year in 1922. When he was first trying out with the Black Sox, he obtained a nickname because of his hitting. He had tremendous power and would hit balls so hard during batting practice, they would make a sound "Boojum!!" when they hit the wall.

The value of his worth early in his career could be summed up by the fact that he was considered to be traded for Martin Dihigo (HOFer), and John Beckwith (a should be HOFer).

If the Hall of Fame has a problem with the selection of Jud Wilson, they need to be put out of business.

27.) Radcliffe, Theodore Roosevelt (Ted Double Duty)
From: 1928-50 Positions: **C, P,** Manager
Teams: Detroit Stars, St Louis Stars, Homestead Grays, Pittsburgh Crawfords, Columbia Blue Birds, Cleveland Giants, New York Black Yankees, Bismark North Dakota, Chicago American Giants, Cincinnati Tigers, Memphis Red Sox, Birmingham Black Barons, Kansas City Monarchs, Harlem Globetrotters, and the Louisville Buckeyes.

The player I compare "Double Duty" to was HOFer Bullet Joe Rogan. Not because of his style of play, but because of his eclecticism.

Rogan was not just exceptional as a pitcher, but as an outfielder. Double Duty's name was an indication as to what he did. He was exceptional as a catcher and as a pitcher. Double-headers were made for Double Duty Radcliffe.

The colorful player was fortunate enough to have played with, and help to guide two great teams, the 1931 Homestead Grays, and the 1932 Pittsburgh Crawfords.

As a pitcher, his ledger indicated a 66-34 record. His lifetime B. A. was .289. Double Duty played for 23 years. He was always in demand as a player because of his abilities.

<u>CATEGORY II</u>

I call them the twilight zone players. The player who split the time between the Negro Leagues and the status quo leagues, and could not combine his efforts (visible to the HOF committee) through no fault of his own.

He possibly spent unwarranted time in the minor leagues. Players such as Roy Campanella, and Monte Irwin were able to satisfy the committee. The following players were not, but I consider them Hall of Fame players anyway.

*Larry Doby was originally selected by me in 1997, but was recently selected (1998) by the committee.

1.) <u>Boyd, Robert Richard (Bob, The Rope)</u>
From: 1946-50 Position: <u>**IB**</u>
Team: Memphis Red Sox

Bob Boyd first played baseball in the Negro Leagues with the Memphis Red Sox. The lefthander first baseman played four years in the Negro Leagues accumulating a lifetime B, A. of .362. with the Red Sox, his only NL team.

In 1950, Bob became the first Black player signed by the Chicago White Sox. Instead of letting him play on the apparent team, he was sent down to the minor leagues.

His records in the NL didn't seem to matter to the White Sox. He was 30 years old before he was given a "chance and opportunity" to play in the major leagues. After all we are only talking about three years after Jackie (1947), and the American League was not ready for too many African-American players.

He was the first Oriole to hit .300. Bob also played winter ball in Latin America obtaining a lifetime B. A. for 4 years of over .300.

Bob's line drive hits earned him the nickname of "The Rope." He ended his major league career of nine years with a .293 batting average. A Joe Morgan type hitter, he belongs in the HOF. For the lack of opportunity time was wasted in the minor leagues.

2.) <u>Doby, Lawrence Eugene (Larry, LD) a.k.a. Larry Walker</u>
From: 1942-47 (Military Service '44-'45)   Positions: <u>**2B,**</u> 3B, Team: Newark Eagles

In his first year, this lefthander power hitting second baseman hit .341 for the champion Newark Eagles. In his third season in the Negro Leagues the homerun leaders were Josh Gibson, and Johnny Davis. They were tied and finished one homerun ahead of Larry.

In 1947, he left his .414 batting average to join the Cleveland Indians. He and Satchel Paige would lead the Cleveland team to the pennant, and on to the championship. Larry hit .301 for the season, and .318 for the series.

Doby spent 13 years in the major leagues with a dream HOF career. Larry hit 253 homeruns, had five 100 RBI seasons, and led the major leagues in homeruns twice, and was the batting champion once.

In 1947, if they had taken all of the Negro League stars, which played with major caliber teams, and signed them on major league rosters, the story on the history of the game would be a lot different.

It appeared that there were too many Negro League stars that displayed the ability of super stardom in both leagues to be ignored, Doby was one of them.

3.) <u>Howard, Elston (Gene, Ellie)</u>
From: 1948-50 Mil. Serv. 1950-52, 1952-68 (major leagues) Positions: <u>C,</u> OF, IB
Teams: Kansas City Monarchs (NL), New York Yankees, Boston Red Sox.

In the three years Howard played with the Kansas City Monarchs (1948, '49, '50) as a catcher and an outfielder, he hit .283, .270, and .319.

Howard should have never gone to the minor leagues. It was really a time for the status quo league to give if the Negro Major League's stars their time. This is particularly true around the time Ellie came out of the service in 1952, because the NL teams were depleting.

Jackie's start (1947) had proven what they were capable of doing…so why change the pattern?

If in fact the Negro Major Leagues were playing major league caliber baseball, then Howard and the other players that fit into this category did not need the extra scrutiny.

Howard was one of the Yankee's top players for 13 years. He finished his last year with the Boston Red Sox in 1968.

The powerful right-handed hitter hit .290 for a lifetime B. A. in the Negro Leagues, and a .274 B. A. in the major leagues. Howard's ability as a player was never properly evaluated, because he shared playing time with Yogi Berra. The problem was solvable.

4.) <u>Minoso, Saturiino Orestes Arrieta Armas (Minnie)</u>
From: 1945-45 (NL) 1949,1951-64, '76, '80)
Teams: New York Cubans, Chicago White Sox, Cleveland Indians, St Louis Cardinals, and the Washington Senators.

This talented young Cuban had a bright future, after hitting .313 in 3of his first 4 years with the New York Cubans.

He was the leadoff man in 1946, and led the Cubans to the Negro National League pennant, and the "World Series." He was the starting 3rd baseman for the 1947 and '48 East-West Star games.

Even though the Cleveland Indians signed him, Minnie spent most of 15 years with the Chicago White Sox. The fleet-footed Minoso was switched to the outfield, and led the America League in stolen bases for his first three full seasons.

For 15 years or more, Minoso always hit around .300. He hit 186 homeruns, and stole over 200 bases. He had a lifetime B. A. of .298. There are players in the HOF who didn't produce those stats.

Minnie was another player I feel was bounced around in the minor leagues unnecessarily. He spent over three productive years with a NML team, and led the New York Cubans to the pennant and the "World Series."

Considering what he did do before and after being sent to the minor leagues, was it really necessary? Even without a look-see?

For endurance, Minoso was asked to be a five-decade player. The Chicago White Sox brought him back in 1976 as a pinch hitter, and 1980.

Starting in 1965, he played in Mexico for nine addition seasons. His last season at age 50, he hit .265 in 1973.

### 5.)	**<u>Newcombe, Donald (Don, Newk)</u>**
From:	1946-49 NL, 1949-51 ML, 1952-53 Military, 1954-60 ML
Positions: **<u>P, PH.</u>**
Teams: Newark Eagles-NL, Brooklyn Dodgers, Los Angeles Dodgers, Cincinnati Reds, and the Cleveland Indians.

During my teenage years, Don Newcombe was the most dominant pitcher in the National League, possibly the majors. The big right-hander had the power of a Nolan Ryan, and the grace and velocity of a Bob Gibson.

I recall a time when Newcombe threw so hard, until he singed Roy Campanella's glove hand. Needless to say, as a young Black youth playing baseball in high school, he was the one most admired by me, as a pitcher.

As a 19-year-old in 1945 with the Newark Eagles, he was 8-3, and had that blazing fastball. Manager Walt Alston often used Newk at 6 feet 4 inches tall and over 200 pounds, as a pinch-hitter. He was very effective. I think one year he hit 8 homeruns.

I believe that Don Newcombe spent unwarranted time in the minor leagues. From 1946-49 in the NL, but from 1949-51 in the minors (military time '52-'53). Big Newk with the very high kick motion was "the man." He was the best pitcher in baseball in the 50's to me.

His best season was in 1956, when he went 27-7, and won the CY Young Award, and the Most Valuable Player Award in the National League. A feat that is a rarity today for a pitcher.

Don Newcombe finished his career with a 149-90 ledger (62%), and a 3.56 ERA. He should have already been placed in the HOF.

///

CATEGORY III

This category is made up of those NL players who were denied "chance and opportunity" in the early stages of professional baseball, or played for a short period of time due to injury, or early death, or were denied "chance and opportunity" after the "color line" because of age, and finally racism.

1.) <u>Allen, Newton Henry (Newt, Colt)</u>
Active From: 1922 to 1944 & 1947   Position: 2B, SS, 3B, OF, IB, Manager
Teams: All Nations, Kansas City Monarchs, St Louis Stars, Detroit Wolves, Homestead Grays, and the Indianapolis Clowns.

J. L. Wilkinson discovered this super star second baseman in 1921 with the Omaha Federals. At the time, Wilkinson owned the All Nations team, and the Kansas City Monarchs. The Monarchs being the major team. He put Allen on the All Nations team, but he did not stay there long. In 1922, he was elevated to the Monarchs.

As captain of the Monarchs, Newt helped the team win pennants in 1923, '24, '25, and '29.

In 1924, the first "World Series" was held between winners from the NNL and the ECL. The Monarchs won a hard fought best of nine game series led by Newt's .282 average and 7 doubles.

For a period of seven seasons (1924-30), Newt's averages were .277, .308, .259, .334, .280, .330, and .345. In 1931, Newt signed with the St Louis Stars where he was teamed with HOF player Willie Wells to create what some experts say was the best double-play combo in baseball at that time. In 1931, he hit .274, and .326 in 1932.

Newt was a "Gold Glove" performer with a very wide range. In fact, he was considered the best 2nd baseman in the 1920's and the early '30's.

Newt Allen completed his career in the NL with a batting average of .296. He also had a .301 B. A. against the status quo players. If a player today spends 23 years in the major leagues, and has a .296 B. A. and was the type of hitter Newt was he would have at least 3,000 hits. The Hall was made for him.

2.) <u>Barnhill, David (Dave, Impo, Skinny)</u>
Active From: 1937 to l949 Position: <u>P.</u>
Teams: Zula Giants, Ethiopian Clowns, and the New York Cubans.

Dave Barnhill was one of the great pitchers of the NL. He was denied "chance and opportunity" twice by the status quo. The first time was when he was going to be the first Black player in the status quo major leagues.

He received a telegram from the owner of the Pittsburgh Pirates, Ben Benswanger. Dave and Roy Campanella were supposed to have a tryout. However, Benswanger changed his mind.

The second "Hope Unborn" time was after Dave led the New York Cubans to a "World Series" victory in 1947. He also led the league in victories (13), and a 2.81 ERA. One would think that after a super star had had that kind of a season, he would be signed and welcomed into the status quo major leagues.

Particularly, after the season Jackie and Doby proved what was possible of becoming a reality…A fusion of the two leagues.

The New York Giants signed Dave along with HOFer Ray Dandrige. However, they were immediately sent down to the Giants AAA club, Minneapolis…Mistake!!

Just imagine, two superstars of the NL, and still productive, and not given a chance to show their greatness, but degraded and demoted.

Barnhill, trying to make the best of it had an 11-3 season to help the AAA club team to their championship. He was accused of doctoring the ball, then when that accusation failed, they accused Dandrige of helping him, but Dandrige maintain his innocence.

In the early 40's, the small fastballer was the top pitcher in the East, and represented them in All-Star games against Satchel Paige. Dave and Satchel split games against each other. In 1941 he recorded a ledger of 18-3, and 26-10 in 1943.

3.) <u>Easter, Luscious (Luke)</u>
From; 1947-48 (NML), 1949-1954 (major leagues) Positions: <u>OF, IB</u>
Teams: Homestead Grays and the Cleveland Indians

This 6' 4 ½" 240 pounds of power was a Willie McCovey type hitter. Luke did not just hit homeruns, but tape measured ones. I remember reading stories in the Pittsburgh Courier about some of the monstrous homeruns that he hit in different stadiums.

I feel that Luke Easter was a victim of the status quo. A budding star at the dawn of the new day for NL players after the "color line." This was a great opportunity for the status quo to be equitable, and make the transition as good as it should/could have been. Here's what happen to Luke.

Luke started as a rookie with the Gray's in 1947. He was supposed to be the next Josh Gibson. Because Buck Leonard (now in the HOF) was the first baseman, the rookie Easter had to play in the outfield.

He responded with a .382 B. A., and 43 homeruns. The following year, (1948) he hit .403 for the last pennant for the Grays, and he was selected for the East-West all-star game.

In 1949, the Cleveland Indians signed Luke Easter. He was sent to the farm without seeing what he could do. He had already been productive on a Negro major league team. He was sent down to San Diego in the Pacific Coast League. Luke responded with a .363 B. A., and 25 homeruns in only 80 games.

The following year (1950), he was invited to Cleveland to be a rookie again. He played first base, hit .280, and had 28 homeruns. In 1951, he hit 27 HRS, in 1952 he hit 31 homeruns.

In 1953, Luke broke his foot, but still hit .303. The next year, he spent part of a season pinch-hitting. He never really got the chance to play in the major leagues again.

Luke made the best of his minor league career, and ended up with a .296 lifetime B. A. He had a .274 lifetime major league batting average, and a .336 lifetime batting average in the Negro Leagues. According to my totals, I could only account for Luke hitting in all competition for 17 years.

He hit at least 553 homeruns. I believe Luke's talents were denied in the fullest potential, and he would have been a HOFer without question.

4.) <u>Fowler, John W. (Bud) a.k.a. John W. Jackson (his real name)</u>
From: 1878-1904 Positions: **<u>2B, P</u>**, SS, 3B, OF, C, Manager
Teams: Page Fence Giants, Cubans Giants, Smoky City Giants, All-American Black Tourists, Kansas City Stars.

In the early days of professional baseball, there was no "color line." Bud Fowler played organized baseball with White leagues on White teams. He did this until the "color line," or "gentlemen's agreement" came about.

In 1887, Bud Fowler was dropped from the Binghamton team of the International League and was not allowed to sign with other teams in the league…"chance and opportunity."

Bud was the first professional Black baseball player in 1878. His best position was second base, but he was also a good pitcher.

After pitching for Stillwater in 1884, Bud did not pitch much after that. Fowler was forced off several teams by White teammates who didn't want him there.

So Bud organized the Page Fence Giants, an all Black team. Bud was the manager and 2nd baseman. Grant "Homerun" Johnson was the shortstop. Bud hit .316, and the team had a 118-36 record. Later that year, he played with Lansing in the Michigan State League, and hit .331 while playing 2nd and 3rd. Bud stated that he had played with teams based in 22 states and Canada.

Bud Fowler, one of the brave early American heroes. For a time in history, he stood alone as a single voice for African-Americans and their opportunity and place in professional baseball. He has every right to be in the HOF.

There are other stars in the HOF who played, and had opportunity in that era because they were members of the status quo league. Bud was denied his true chance, but demonstrated his abilities.

He was allowed to play before the "color line" in a limited capacity on some good teams. It was not Bud's fault that he did not get the opportunity to participate because of the color of his skin. The HOF has an obligation to let him in.

5.) <u>Grant, Ulysses F. (Frank)</u>

From: 1889-1905 (Negro Leagues), 1886-88, '90- Other leagues

Positions: **<u>2B</u>,** SS, P, OF, 3B, C.

Teams: Buffalo Bisons, Cuban Giants, New York Gorhams, Colored Capital All-Americans, New York Big Gorhams, Page Fence Giants, Cubans X-Giants, Philadelphia Giants, and the Genuine Cuban Giants.

This right-handed hitting speedster was said to be the best professional baseball player of the nineteenth century. Because he was a second baseman, he was called the "Black Dunlap." This was because Fred Dunlap was considered to be the best White second baseman of the 1880's.

Frank Grant batted .366 and stole 40 bases for the Buffalo Bisons in 1887. Those are very good statistics, but his teammates didn't want to take team photos with him.

Imagine what problems he must have had on a social level? If he experienced these problems with his teammates, think of what happened with opposing players?

In 1888, Frank hit .346, but he was refused a contract the following year.

What player today (money not being a factor), hits .346, and 11 homeruns in a full season and is denied a contract the following year?

"Why the runners chased him (Grant) off second base. They went down so often trying to break his legs or injure him that he gave up his infield position the latter part of last season and played right field.

About half the pitchers try their best to hit these colored players when they are at bat. I know of a great many pitchers that tried to soak Grant."

—The Sporting News 1889

Despite racial insults, "kill the Nigger," shouted one fan during a game, and injures from opposing players trying to hurt him. He i.e. Bud Fowler maintained outstanding composure and statistics in spite of great obstacles.

Before the 1890's, the "color line" was raised in most White leagues, forcing Fowler, Grant, and other outstanding NL players to form their own teams.

In 1889, like so many other inventions, because of the need to avoid injuries, Frank Grant according to some experts has been given credit for the invention of shin guards.

Roger Bresnahan, a status quo league player has also been given this credit, but he did not become a regular player until 1901 with Baltimore. Roger started his career as a pitcher, then became a star center fielder. Later in his career, which ended in 1915, he became a catcher, and that would be the only reason for him to use shin guards.

Grant started with the Bisons in 1889, and because of the nature of the position he played (second base), it created a special reason for shin guards. Frank also played shortstop and spent time as a catcher, but his major position was second base.

As attested by The Sporting News, Frank Grant's mission to be the best he could be was snuffed out by the status quo. Now he should get the chance.

6.) <u>Jones, Stuart (Slim)</u>
From: 1932-38 Position: <u>**P**</u>
Teams: Baltimore Black Sox, and the Philadelphia Stars.

This tall slender southpaw dominated Black baseball in the mid-30's. He was always among the leaders in strikeouts with an overpowering fast ball, and an outstanding curveball. In 1934, Jones had a 32-4 season in his third year for the Philadelphia Stars.

He pitched the Stars to the league championship, and finally to a 2-0 shutout over the Chicago American Giants to win the championship. To close out the 1934 season, Jones beat Dizzy Dean, a HOF pitcher, and the "World Champion," St. Louis Cardinals.

Slim Jones, was 6' ft. 6", and 185 pounds. He was selected for the 1934 and 1935 East-West All Star games. The matches between Jones and Satchel Paige were legendary.

One of their most famous matches came in Yankee Stadium in 1934. This game went 10 innings and ended in a 1-1 tie, because of darkness. Some experts proclaim this game to be the best in Black baseball. Jones had a no-hitter for 6 innings. He gave up 3 hits while striking out 9. Satchel gave up 6 hits, and struck out 12.

HOFer Buck Leonard faced both Jones and Lefty Grove. Leonard said that Jones was faster. Most experts believe that Jones threw as fast or faster than Paige did.

Jones had a short career and life, but proved his abilities. He had a drinking problem, and he had arm problems. He died of pneumonia in 1938 at the young age of 25, but played in the Negro Major Leagues with Baltimore and Philadelphia for seven years.

7.) <u>**Smith, Charles (Charlie, Chino)**</u>
From: 1924-31 Positions: <u>**OF,**</u> 2B.
Teams: Philadelphia Giants, Pennsylvania Red Caps of New York, Brooklyn Royal Giants, and the New York Lincoln Giants.

Satchel Paige claimed that this little fleet-footed outfielder was one of the two greatest hitters in the Negro Leagues…Jud Wilson is the other. They have not been considered for the HOF.

Hall of Fame voters are you listening? If you can't get a vote of approval from the general recognized "best pitcher" to come out of the Negro Leagues, who can you depend on?

Chino is given credit for the highest batting average in the Negro Leagues at .469. He was given the nickname "Chino" because of his slanted eyes.

As a left-handed hitter who always intimidating pitchers, Chino was a line drive "Pete Rose" type hitter with power who rarely struck out. Experts say he had no weakness as a hitter.

Smith hit third in the line-up of the powerful New York Lincoln Giants. He was a superior hitter, and proved it in a short eight years of his Negro League career.

Chino hit for a lifetime Negro League B. A. of .423, and a .420 lifetime batting average against the status quo. In 1929, Chino hit .464, and had 23 homeruns to lead the American Negro League in both categories.

In January of 1932, Smith fell sick and died. It was thought to have been the yellow fever. Chino died before he turned 30 years of age. He spent eight years in the Negro Leagues.

8.) <u>**Stovey, George Washington**</u>
From: 1886-96 Positions <u>**P,**</u> OF.
Teams; Cuban Giants, New York Gorhams, Cuban X-Giants, Jersey City, Newark, and the Brooklyn Colored Giants.

While Fleetwood Walker was the first professional major league African-American baseball player, and Bud Fowler was the first African-American professional baseball player, and George Stovey became the first Black professional baseball player from New Jersey after he was kidnapped from the Cuban Giants.

George Stovey, a great left-handed pitcher, won 33 games for Newark in 1887. He reportedly could have pitched for any team at that time in the country…race not being a factor.

In 1887, George was scheduled to pitch against HOF inducted Cap Anson's Chicago White Stockings with Fleetwood Walker (an African-American) as the catcher, and the first Black battery.

Cap Anson, the manager took this action. He announced that his team would not be taking the field to play if the two Black players were allowed to take the field. Of course, they were denied "chance and opportunity" to realize their true potentials not only in the game, but their careers.

After Stovey was kidnapped, he defeated his former teammates twice, and won 30 games with Jersey City as he held opponents to a .167 batting average. Because of these performances, the New York Giants owner, Appleton wanted to sign him, but did not probably because of known feelings of a racial nature around the league.

After the incident with Cap Anson, the International League leadership met and decided that it was now time for the "color line" to be established in their league. However, Stovey continued to pitch with Newark until the end of the season with a 34-15 ledger. He also played some in the outfield and hit .255.

When Newark released Stovey that September, he returned to the Cuban Giants, and accumulated a 60-40 record, and a 2.17 ERA in organized baseball. How can the HALL not be tempted?

END OF CATEGORY III

We would have known what real major league baseball was all about.

"The Course of Time" needs to start and take place with the HOF voters. I don't believe that Black/minorities and players today are particularly denied induction into the HOF because of race. I don't want to believe that, however, players are still denied for inconsistent reasons.

I don't buy the reasons given by some writers having to refuse induction of some eligible players: (1) The player did not dominate the game at his position, (2) Winning 300 games is not that hard anymore, (3) He didn't win the Cy Young award, or MVP, and (4) He didn't play long enough.

While number one is a legitimate reason, "domination of the game" in ones position is not always what is used in each evaluation. The committee needs to decide on whether to use this or not. First though, they need to define what they mean by domination. Was he first for a specified time, his career or in the top two or three? The best or amongst the best? This is an example of what I mean.

Sandy Koufax and Don Drysdale played relatively the same time. In fact, they pitched for the same team...you guessed it, my Dodger Blues. They were both dominant pitchers and deserving HOF recognition, which they did receive.

The question is, assuming that they were eligible at the same time, should Koufax be accepted into the HOF because he was more dominant than Drysdale, or vice versa? Should one be first just to make the other one wait? And why should a player wait?

If they met the standards of previous HOFers, they shouldn't have problems getting into the HOF. However, if we theorize that it has to be one or the other then one deserving player will not get in at that time and maybe never. Why? Because those are the unwritten rules.

Don Sutton was first placed on the ballot in 1993 with a "dominant" pitcher, Steve Carlton. The only dominant difference between Steve Carlton and Don Sutton was a faster fast ball. Carlton did win 20 games six times, but Sutton won 324 games in 23 years. Carlton won 319 games in 24 seasons. Carlton had 55 shutouts, and Sutton had 58. The league hit .236 against Sutton, and .240 against Carlton.

So you say, where is more consistency that makes Sutton the equal to Carlton? Here it is, Sutton won at least 17 games 7 times, and he won at least 15 games 12 times, that plus the other facts I mentioned.

Somebody tell me why Steve Carlton goes into the HOF in the first year, and Sutton had to wait several times more? I don't want to hear about Sutton offended certain writers during the time he was playing baseball. What does that have to do with his role on the field?

You want to talk domination at a position? Most writers and baseball historians will agree that Nolan Ryan was one of the most dominant pitchers of his time, or anytime, but it took Ryan 27 years to win 323 games and Sutton only 23. Nolan won 20 games only twice, and never won a CY Young award.

Nolan Ryan did not have to wait to get into the HOF, and he shouldn't have. After all, that is my point. The proof of Nolan's mastery of the game is his endurance. Apparently, this not a quality that is admired by some HOF voting writers with certain players, but it is by others.

(2) "Winning 300 games is not that hard," then why do we have pitchers (not including players retired because of injury, or relievers) in the HOF with less than 300 game wins? There are 62 pitchers in the HOF at this writing, 98% of them were starters.

Sutton is tied for the 12th spot with the most wins of all time; it would mean that over 45 pitchers already in the HOF at this writing found it hard to win 300 games. What about the pitchers who fell between 200 and 300 games, why don't we ask them that question? Winning 300 games takes perseverance, endurance, health, talent, and "chance and opportunity"…enough said.

Let's go to number four. "He didn't play long enough." For this phrase, we need to look at the total player.

Bruce Sutter won a CY Young award, dominated the game as a reliever from 1979 to 1984 (6 years), and obtained a career threaten injury. There are great players already in the HOF whose careers were shorten by injuries. Players like Sandy Koufax, Dizzy Dean, and Roy Campanella, just to mention three…So that precedence has already been set up.

Not only was Sutter dominating from 1979 to 1984, he revolutionized baseball and introduced a new pitch in the process, the split-finger fastball. Now starters and relievers in all of baseball are using the pitch.

There has never been a reliever more dominating than Sutter in that span of time. He saved 300 games in 12 years. Rollie Fingers, Hoyt Wilhelm (both in the HOF), or even Lee Smith in a longer period of time were never more dominating or changed the game of baseball more.

Someone said that imitation was the greatest form of flattery. Youngsters and young prospects alike imitated Sutter. He had more success with his followers with the split-finger fastball than Wilhelm did with the knuckleball, because the knuckleball was harder to control. However, Sutter was just as successful, but in a shorter span of time.

Major leaguers hit .230 lifetime against Sutter, and they hit .236 against Rollie Fingers, and Lee Smith. Sutter is not even considered for the HOF. The HOF is the loser when they overlook this type situation, and make bad decisions such as this.

One voter said, "I gave my opinion, but this is nothing personal." If it's nothing personal, we should just look at the facts. If its nothing personal, we should look at the prospective HOFers and compare them to the present HOFers. This is more evidence why the HOF voting or criterion needs to be updated…very soon.

This also shows proof that "Hope Unborn" is not just pertaining to the roots of my past, and African-Americans, but it affects all Americans whether they recognized it or not.

Some HOFers had to wait 15 years for the veterans committee to free them, and do what should have been done years earlier i.e. Nellie Fox, Jim Bunning, and Larry Doby. Maybe the answer is to allow the veteran's committee to vote in the first place, or the second time around.

I want to strongly express that the players in the Negro Leagues were more like the players today in terms of quality, because they followed the money, and opportunity. The status quo players were more bound to contract. Free agency first existed in the Negro Leagues. Think about it.

The Negro League stars were not bound by contract like the status quo players then and unlike today. They would leave their teams in the middle of the season for more money.

Satchel Paige, Josh Gibson, and other NL players were paid greatly to leave their current teams to travel to Mexico, Cuba, or even teams in the other leagues across the country.

In fact, in 1943, the St. Louis Stars withdrew from the Negro National League to barnstorm with Dizzy Dean & Company. The league suspended them of course, but the move did take place.

The "course of time" for baseball is now. I would like to challenge the major leagues of baseball in America to be the leading country to organize, or propose organization for professional inter-globe baseball similar to what is mentioned in the book.

This would make baseball in America fair and more legitimate in the their assessment of what baseball truly is. Let's give more validity to the meaning of words like "All-Star game, All-Stars, World Series, and the Hall of Fame."

Let baseball in America be the first sport to come against racial type stereo names like the Indians, Braves, Reds, or Redskins, and others that promote ethnological practices in our country. Baseball is the game I love, and I would love to see baseball lead the way toward what America should be about.

CHAPTER VII—VOTING FOR GREATNESS
THE ALL-20TH CENTURY BASEBALL TEAM

When I considered that an All-Century team would be named at the 1999 "World Series," I delayed the closure of my book.

I discovered that two All-Century teams would be named. One on NBC by Bob Costas before game time, and another one just before the game on the field another team would be introduced by one of my all-time Dodger Blues, Vin Scully. Master Card featuring some living legends at the Ted (Turner Stadium) minutes before the game sponsored this one.

Once again, the players from the Negro Leagues were snuffed out. Bob Costas named none of the great Negro players on NBC. However, of the 30 players named by Costas, 10 players were from the status quo league. How is this justified?

Let me understand this reasoning. One third of the players voted on for the best in all of baseball for the past 100 years are players who played in a segregated league? And further more, these "best players" played during a time when there were other players of the same quality in another league, but were not allowed to play with these "best players?" How can this be justified?

I have to believe that this is possible only because of the lack of education of the voters.

From the top 25 "players of the century" voted on by fans through Master Card, seven of those players were basically from the status quo league and once again no representation from the Negro Leagues.

After the report on NBC by Costas, he apologized to the fans for the omission of Satchel Paige, Josh Gibson, and some of the other NL stars he felt should have been there. That's because Bob Costas knows some of the real history of the Negro Leagues.

The apology was fine in a status quo sort of way, but it did nothing to correct the real problems concerning baseball today, which continues throughout the baseball community in America. It's like locking the barn after the horse is out.

Had the organizers of this wonderful idea had the insight and respect of good will for our "national past time," prior organizational planning would have gone into it. Such as, how to educate the fans on the history of baseball in the past one hundred years?

All baseball, Black and White should be apart of our knowledge of the game. Some of us might be uncomfortable with it, but it's history, and by doing so the facts are released. We should be concerned by some of the more important things that happened in history.

Had it not been for the exposure of Black and Hispanic players, Robinson, Doby, Mays, Aaron, and Banks would have continued the journey they started buried in the NL as has been by the greats before them. As it was, only Bob Gibson and Ken Griffey, Jr. were included in this uninformed voting. Only Mays, Aaron, Banks, and Robinson had any ties to the Negro Leagues.

<u>INAPPROPIATE BEHAVIOR</u>

The night seemed to be captured by Jim Gray, the NBC reporter who received most of the attention when he cornered Pete Rose, and appeared focussed on embarrassing him for coming out to acknowledge and celebrate his part of the all-century team.

More befitting would have been to ask Pete about his health, or how did he feel about coming back, or being welcomed by the fans? Or why not ask him about the selection of certain players? Many appropriate things could have been discussed, and probably welcomed by all concerned.

Getting a confession out of Pete Rose, which I think Gray realizes by now, should not have been his top priority. I don't think Rose should be challenged on this point for Hall of Fame purposes, but assuming that he should be, this was not the proper forum.

What I really want the readers to know is that we have allowed racists, convicted drug abusers, womanizers, and other law breakers to be accepted into the good graces of our "national past time."

None of us is perfect and second chances have been apart of our culture. I suppose this is true except when it comes to Rose, and the 14 other players ban for life, and a certain group of dark skin Americans before 1950 or thereabouts. If you compare this area to other sports, you will see where baseball is wrong.

<u>WHAT ELSE IS WRONG WITH THE CURRENT SELECTION?</u>

I fail to see how 25 or 30 players, would be an adequate number of satisfaction for the top players of the last 100 years. Particularly if none of the players from the Negro Leagues are considered. I would have trouble with that limited number just in the African-Americans/dark skin Hispanics alone. I think it has to be a minimum of at least 40, and a maximum of 50 players. My total was 46.

Now I will name my all-century team…if that's possible and it will be based on my research, first-hand experience, and knowledge of the 45 players that I believe should be selected from <u>ALL OF AMERICAN MAJOR LEAGUE BASEBALL COMPETITION</u> for the past 100 years.

*Comments are only made on those Negro League players who are not discussed in Chapter VI, and were not named on the NBC/Master Card teams:

CATCHERS
*Josh Gibson
Johnny Bench
Roy Campanella

FIRST BASEMEN
Mark McGwire
*Buck Leonard
Lou Gehrig

SECOND BASEMAN
*John Henry Lloyd
Jackie Roosevelt Robinson
Roger Hornsby
Joe Morgan

SHORTSTOPS
Ernie Banks
Dick Lundy
Cal Ripken, Jr.
Honus Wagner

THIRD BASEMAN
Mike Schmidt
Jud Wilson
Brooks Robinson

PITCHERS
Sandy Koufax
*Satchel Paige
Nolan Ryan
Bob Gibson
Jose` Mendez
Cy Young
Walter Johnson
Nip Winters
Warren Spahn
Tom Seaver
Lefty Grove
Smokey J. Williams

OUTFIELDERS
Hank Aaron
*Oscar Charleston
Willie Howard Mays
Christobol Torriente
George Herman Ruth
Ted Williams
Norman "Turkey" Stearns
Charles "Chino" Smith
Pete "Charlie Hustle" Rose
Ricky Henderson
Ty Cobb
Spottswood Poles
Tony Gwynn

Roberto Clemente`
Mickey Mantle
Ken Griffey, Jr.
Joe DiMaggio

<u>THE STARTING LINEUP—ALL 20th CENTURY TEAM</u>

IB—Mark McGwire
2B—John Henry Lloyd
SS—Richard "Dick" Lundy
3B—Mike Schmidt
C—Josh Gibson
Outfielders—Hank Aaron
Willie Mays
Oscar Charleston
Pitchers (LHP)—Sandy Koufax
Satchel Paige

The author selected as all-century players the following list of Negro League players, and they have not been introduced properly as characters in this book. Hopefully, this small write up on some of their history will help you understand their selection.

(1.) <u>Walter Fenner "Buck" Leonard</u>—Position: IB, 1933-50

As a powerful hitting first baseman mostly for the Homestead Grays, Leonard was a left-handed hitter. Buck, it seems for some reason is one of the players from the Negro Leagues that is always compared to the best status quo player of his day at first base. In this case it was Lou Gehrig.

He was the clean-up hitter for one of the most powerful Negro League teams from 1937 to 1945. Buck was hitter extraordinare for the Homestead Gray's "murderers row." Josh Gibson and Buck were compared to Ruth and Gehrig.

It was said, "trying to sneak a fastball past him was like trying to sneak a sunrise past a roster."

Buck hit from 1939 to 1945 .363, .372, .275, .265, .327, .290, and .375. for those championship years. During the 40's, he averaged over 34 homeruns per year, while playing between 50 to 60 games a year.

Smokey Joe Williams discovered him playing with the Brooklyn Royal Giants, and made arrangements for him to play with the Grays from 1934 to 1950.

Buck was selected by Cum Posey on the all-time All-American team. Cum stated that Buck was in a class by himself as a fielder and a hitter.

In over 17 years in the Negro National Leagues, Buck Leonard had a lifetime batting average of .341, and an average of .382 in exhibition games against the status quo major leaguers.

Buck appeared in eleven all-star classics (a record), and compiled a lifetime batting average of .317. He also won three batting titles.

In 1939, Clark Griffith, the owner of the Washington Senators called Buck and Josh Gibson into his office to see if they were interested in playing for his team. They agreed to give it a try, but nothing came of it.

Later, Bill Veeck offered him a chance at age 44 with the St. Louis Browns (1952), but he knew his skills on that level had diminished and he declined the offer.

In 1955, at the closing of a 23-year career totally in baseball, Buck went south of the border at the tender age of 48 and hit 13 homeruns, and batted .312 in 62 games with Durango in the Central Mexican League.

(2.) **Robert LeRoy "Satchel" Paige**—Position: Pitcher, 1926-1967

Quite possibly the greatest pitcher to darn a baseball uniform in the 20th century. How do you give credentials and specify the greatness of a legend when he is beyond words? The second and third hand experiences and knowledge that I have of Satchel is enough to give him credibility in my book. No, I did not see Satchel pitch in his prime, but I have friends who did.

I never thought that anyone would have to defend Satchel Paige, a legend in Black baseball, and subsequently a legend in American and Central American baseball. To have to justify to the American public why he should be ranked among the top two pitchers of the 20th century not to mention being named to the team, smacks of ignorance by our fans, which is not necessarily their fault. Would you ask a citizen to vote on a candidate he/she has no knowledge of? Of course not…the same reasoning applies here.

I was under the impression that Satchel Paige was at least as much a household name as Jackie Robinson. Based on the voting, I see I was misinformed. This is how the domino effect of Satchel Paige reached me even though I didn't see him.

At 15 going on 16, I was a junior and a prospective sensational high school pitcher. Cecil Clark, a childhood friend of mine, was already a senior, and an established pitcher in and around Lakeland, Florida with American Legion teams. Cecil was almost unhittable. Our high school (Rochelle) was not due to get a team until the next year (1957-58).

With this in mine, I wanted Cecil to avail me of all the knowledge he had about pitching. I was excited for him and enjoyed watching him make hitters look silly with his hesitation pitch. He did not care what the count was; he would use it in any situation.

Cecil imparted all of his knowledge about pitching to me except one thing, the hesitation pitch. He told me that Satchel taught our homeboy Squab (Jimmy "Squab" Hill, formerly of the Newark Eagles) how to throw it. According to Cecil, Squab taught it to him. It was a pitch that I wanted real badly, but Cecil never showed it to me.

In 1948, the Cleveland team's bullpen door swung open, and out came the tall lean 6' 4" 180 pound Paige. He was put together seemingly with screws and tape. The right hander had had a very productive and unbelievable long career in the Negro Leagues.

From 1948, Satchel pitched from the age of 42 a total of 179 games with a 3.29 ERA in the major leagues, as we know it today. Here is a break down on the teams Satchel played with and when.

> Negro Leagues—1926-1948 season
> Cleveland Indians—1948-1949
> St. Louis Browns—1951-1953
> Kansas City Athletics—1965
> *Played in Latin America in between.
> seasons, and later during the season.
> Minor leagues ('56-'58, '65-'66)

In 1965 at age 59, Satchel pitched in his last major league game tossing three shutout innings against the Boston Red Sox for the Kansas City A's.

Joe DiMaggio and Babe Herman made parts of testimonies attributing to the greatness of Paige. Both played against him on the West Coast and said that Satchel was the toughest pitcher they had ever faced.

Paige himself estimated that he pitched over 2,600 games, had 300 shutouts, and 55 no-hitters. Can any pitcher in the last 100 years claim that?

As the oldest rookie to ever play in the status quo major leagues, Paige posted a 6-1 ledger, and a 2.48 ERA down the stretch to help the Cleveland Indians win the pennant and "World Series." At 47, Paige is also the oldest All-Star.

The stories on Satchel Paige are indeed legendary. Some of them I heard as a child, I have yet to investigate the authenticity of some of them.

One story was that when Satchel came to the status quo major leagues, he had to eliminate some of his pitches because certain pitches could not be seen by the umpire properly, caught by the catcher without trouble, or hit by the batter.

As the stories go, it has been reported that Paige use to warm up using a chewing gum wrapper as the plate. Reportedly, one time Satchel was pitching in a game with two men out and one on base. He purposely walked the next two batters to force himself to pitch to Josh Gibson with the bases loaded. He struck Gibson out.

Some of Satchel's teammates claimed that he use to call all of his supporting cast (players) in the infield and sit them down while he struck out the side.

3) **John Henry "Pop" Lloyd (El Cuchara)**—Position: 2B, SS, IB, C, Manager

(Some information already exists in the book about John Henry Lloyd.)

I will begin by saying that George Herman "Babe" Ruth and Honus Wagner stated that John Henry Lloyd was their choice as the greatest player of all time.

Lloyd was described as the greatest player of the first two decades. He excelled at second base, shortstop, and was a great base stealer. He was the complete package in that he could hit, hit with power, run, field, throw, and was good in the clutch.

Lloyd's knowledge of the game allowed him to be very flexible as a player, and later as a manager. He could have easily been placed on the all-century team as a shortstop, but it help to give us more player variety.

Lloyd was not just the greatest Black player of the first two decades, he was the greatest baseball player Black or White. Honus Wagner was his only true comparison until Dick Lundy came along ten years later (1916).

This was attested by John McGraw, Hall of Fame manager the New York Giants who frequented Black baseball games. McGraw made similar statements about Lloyd and Lundy.

About Lloyd McGraw said, "If we could bleach this Lloyd boy, we would show the National League a new phenomenon." What McGraw wanted to do with Lundy was "paint him white." Which would make him palatable to the status quo league, the league McGraw represented.

Lloyd studied hitters, and positioned himself accordingly. He got a great jump on the ball, had a wide and exceptionally long range, sure hands, and dug balls out of the dirt frequently. In fact, his nickname in Cuba where he was a tremendous player was "El Cuchara," which stands for the tablespoon.

The powerful lefthander hitter had a slightly closed stance, which was very productive. He had a lifetime batting average in 27 years of .368. Twelve years lifetime in Cuba produced a batting average of .321 between 1908 and 1930.

Lloyd was one to follow the money, which is something that has not changed. This is why he played for a lot of teams, but most of the time he played with New York teams. Too bad it wasn't the New York Giants.

After completing the 1910 season hitting .417 with the Leland Giants, he returned back east to play with the newly organized New York Lincoln Giants.

At mid-season he took over as manager replacing the great Sol White. The McMahon brothers owned the Giants. For the next three years the Giants were the champions of the East. Lloyd posted batting averages of .475, .376, and .363.

Finally, Babe Ruth had a response when announcer Graham McNamee placed the popular question to him. Ruth was asked who his choice was for the greatest baseball player of all time. He named John Henry Lloyd. How much greater vote and compliment can you get from a player recognized by many as the greatest himself?

4.) <u>Oscar McKinley "Charlie" Charleston</u>—1915-1941 Position: CF, IB, Manager

This six feet one hundred and ninety pound powerful, barrel-chested left-handed hitter was one of the most exciting players of his time. Here again, he was one of the Negro League baseball players often compared with Babe Ruth.

Not only was he compared to Ruth as a hitter, but he was also compared to Ty Cobb as a base stealer and Tris Speaker as an outfielder. As an outfielder, Charleston played as shallow as Andrew Jones of the Atlanta Braves because of his great speed.

Hall of Fame umpire Jocko Conlon said that Oscar was "the greatest Negro Leaguer player of that time."

At 15, Oscar left home and joined the Army. There, he found out he could run very fast. He was timed in the 220-yard dash at 23 seconds. In his youth, he was unparalleled by any player in baseball. Ben Taylor, a star for many years in the NL and one the great NL managers claimed that Charleston was "the greatest outfielder that ever lived…greatest of all colors. He can cover more ground than any man I have ever seen. His judging of fly balls borders on the uncanny." Of course he died in 1953, and his testimony can only cover that period of time.

As a hitter, Charleston hit for average, power, and distance. He used the complete field, and was at his best in the clutch. Take a look at his 1921 season, the second organizational year of the Negro Leagues. In 60 games Oscar hit .434, led the league in stolen bases with 35, hit 14 doubles, 11 triples, and 15 homeruns.

Oscar spent 1932 to 1938 with the team I call the greatest team ever, the Pittsburgh Crawfords. This was also considered much past the age of prime for a baseball player at 36. From 1932 to 1936 Oscar hit .363, .450, .310, .304, and .356, and he was selected to the first three all-star games.

In 27 years of Negro League baseball Oscar Charleston fashioned a lifetime batting average of .357, and hit 151 homeruns. He had a .326 batting average in exhibition games against the status quo players. In nine seasons in the Cuban Winter Leagues, he hit .361.

Finally and rightfully so, he was elected to the Hall of Fame in 1976…possibly, the greatest outfielder and definitely among the greatest players ever.

5.) <u>Joshua "Josh" Gibson</u>   Positions: C, OF, 3B, and IB.

The information already given about Josh in the book qualifies him as the greatest or among the greatest of all-time catchers.

In the NBC's selection, only Johnny Bench, and Yogi Berra were mentioned. In the Master Card selection, Bench and Berra were one and two respectively, while Campanella, and Josh Gibson were fifth and sixth choices with Carlton Fisk as the number four selection.

Most knowledgeable NL fans are aware that Josh hit 962 homeruns in 17 years of NL baseball. What they may not be aware of is that Josh had a lifetime batting average of .354. Gibson hit .412 in exhibition games against the status players. This is some of what Josh did in winter ball.

Mexico—**44 homeruns, .373 BA, 802 slugging %**
Puerto Rico—**13 homeruns (123 at bats), .479 BA, HR every 9.5 at bats, an base hit extra base hit every 4.2 per at bat.**
Cuba—**A .353 BA in two seasons.**
Venezuela—**League folded shortly after it started, went to Veracruz.**
Veracruz—**Hit .467 in ¼ of a season, and missed the homerun title by one HR.**
(Santo Domingo Trujillo)—**Hit .453.**

In addition to his skills as a hitter he had a riffle arm, and was a great receiver. He was quick for a big man and he was a good base runner. None of the catchers voted on had those skills, not even Roy Campanella.

Two of the greatest pitchers from the status quo league endorsed Gibson as their favorite. They were Walter Johnson, and Carl Hubbell. In fact, Walter Johnson appraised Gibson's value (if he were a White player) to be around $200,000. This was twice the value of Bill Dickey, the greatest status quo catcher at that time.

What is also a great testimony of Gibson's greatness is every team that he played on was a winning team, and the players around him became better. All the surviving former teammates of Josh that I have heard gave him the nod as the greatest catcher of all time.

Josh Gibson died at an early age of 35. Reportedly, it was because of a stroke, but Jackie Robinson always felt it was because of so many disappointing times of not being able to get to the status quo major leagues.

Some writers refer to the status quo league as THE major leagues, however, because of the limitations they placed on themselves by not including all players, I feel that it would be wrong to refer to them as THE major leagues when another major league existed as well.

Finally, in 1972, a year after Satchel Paige's induction, Josh Gibson was selected for the HOF.

//

The BBWAA's Big Toy

In 1992, TOPPS magazine (summer issue by Doug Garr) pointed out the unfairness of the Baseball Writers Association of America (BBWAA), because of their historical abilities to overlook quality players…six in particular at that time.

Orlando Cepeda, Phil Rizutto, Al Oliver, Thurman Munson, Jim Bunning, and Allie Reynolds were mentioned as deserving Hall of Fame players. Garr's argument appeared to be the same or similar to mine.

Let's examine why each of these players had not made it to the Hall Of Fame by 1992. Let us see what happened to Orlando Cepeda first. He was a popular player with the fans, but not with the writers especially after problems reportedly related to drugs. His record was compared to Willie "Stretch" McCovey, and he had the numbers.

McCovey hit 521 homeruns in 22 years, and Cepeda hit 379 in 17 seasons. Translation, McCovey average 23.68 homeruns a year, and Cepeda averaged 22.29. At the time of the report Orlando was tied with Tony Perez for the 32nd spot.

Orlando's lifetime batting average is .297, and Willie McCovey's stands at .270. Orlando hit over .300 eight times, Willie only did this feat twice. Orlando had 141 more hits than Willie did in five fewer seasons. They were both "Rookie of the Year," and each player won the MVP award once.

If that seems strange consider this. It was believed that Frank Chance of the Chicago Cubs got into the HOF on the merits of his teammates.

I understand that Al Oliver played mostly with the Pittsburgh Pirates for 18 years, and a lot of people didn't know him. However, we are not talking about most people. We are talking about the BBWAA. If you are a voting member of the BBWAA, and you are placed in a responsible position such voting for potential Hall of Famers, you need to better prepare yourself for that assignment.

You owe that to the people you are considering, their families, and the fans that watched them play, and your readers who are captured by your commentaries as a reporter.

Al Oliver's lifetime batting average was .303. He won a batting title in 1982. He placed 18th on the all-time doubles list (529) ahead of Ruth, Mays and Ted Williams. In 1992, Al Oliver was 36th on the all-time hits list with 2,743. What happened to his selection?

Bunning was compared to the late HOFer Jim "Catfish" Hunter. Hunter pitched on great teams in Oakland, and New York, but look at the comparisons.

Bunning played for "insignificant" teams in Detroit and Philadelphia and did not play in a "World Series." Hunter had five 20-win seasons, and Bunning only had one, but Bunning won 19 games four times, and 17 games 3 other times.

Yet in 17 years Bunning was 224-184, and Hunter was 224-166 in 15 years playing for better teams. Bunning had a lifetime 3.27 ERA, and Hunter's ERA was 3.29. Bunning had 2,855 lifetime strikeouts, while Hunter had 2,012. Bunning led the league in strikeouts 3 times.

According to Garr (TOPPS), "Bunning was easily as good as HOF pitchers Bob Lemon, Rube Marquard, and Red Ruffing."

Thurman Munson's records were seriously compared to Roy Campanella's. Both had their careers shorten, but when Thurman was compared to Ray Schalk, and Rick Ferrell, Munson was criticized because they felt that he didn't play long enough. So why is Dizzy Dean in the HOF? Munson was also introverted, and didn't give many interviews to writers. Do we see a pattern here from the past? I think we do.

Oliver played in small market towns of Pittsburgh, and Montreal. He was not a popular player.

Bunning did not get consideration because his teams were called insignificant. Rizutto, Munson and Reynolds were Yankees, but look how they were treated?

Pee Wee Reese and Phil Ruzutto have similar records. Phil played 13 years, and Pee Wee played 16 years. Phil had a .273 lifetime batting average, while Pee Wee only managed .269. Pee Wee stole 232 bases, and Phil had only 149. Phil scored 887 runs, and Pee Wee had 1,338. Pee Wee also had the edge in RBI at 885 to 562.

It was reported that Rizutto was a "whiner," but because of his similar comparison to Pee Wee Reese his case was made when Pee Wee was voted in.

Apparently, Allie Reynolds had only 13 years going for him even though he was the "Yankee Stopper" in the 40's and 50's. Reynolds lifetime record was 182-107, a .630 winning percentage which ranked him 25th on the all-time list in 1992. Allie had a 3.33 lifetime ERA, two no-hitters, and his post season record was great. He finished at 7-2, 2 shutouts, 4 series saves, and a post-season ERA of 2.79. Maybe he didn't get in because he was a Native American?

Phil Pepe, a former New York Daily News sportswriter and past national president of the BBWAA said, "Writers have told me they simply forget to vote for someone who got in." Yeah right! If this is accurate, the voting writers should have to past some kind of written test pertaining to sportswriters, or some kind of monitored oral test. At least, changes should be made…NOW!

According to Pepe, there are three main considerations for the HOF. They are longevity, dominance at the position in question, and career stats.

The main problem here is that it's too subjective, and not objective.

It would have been interesting to pole the fans at the close of the 1998 baseball season, and tell them of the plan to select the top 100 players of the 20th century.

It would also have been good for baseball to invest on the education of their fans to bring them up to speed with all of baseball in America before 1990. This would have given the fans better voting knowledge, and it would have informed the youngest fan…including information about the Negro Leagues.

Very few fans living today saw Babe Ruth, Ty Cobb, Lou Gehrig, Honus Wagner, Joe Jackson, or many of the great players from the status quo league.

So what makes the fans knowledgeable about their great accomplishments? It's the history presented to them by the media (radio, TV, newspaper, books, magazines), stadiums, books, friends/relatives, and museums.

Commentators making statements on the major network's "game of week" about their memories of the status quo league's players, games, or what made them the great players everyone thought they were.

I have been looking and listening to those reports every since my childhood years. The first time I saw Jackie Robinson, Roy Campanella, and Big Don Newcombe on the baseball field in Lakeland, Florida, my thoughts were…Where are the other Black players on the other teams? And why none of the other teams playing the hated Detroit Tigers had none?

We cannot change the history of American baseball, but we can change our approach by unveiling the total truth about the history of baseball. Somewhere deep down in my utmost thoughts, I really do not think that the people who initiated this wonderful idea wanted the voting public educated about the total history of baseball. Otherwise it would have been better prepared.

It would bring too many skeletons out of the proverbial closet. It would mean that the stars of the past might have had a different past.

Hank Aaron, Maury Wills, Curt Flood, and other Black players sought out to do what the Lord gave them abilities to do, and they were met with obstacles that should not have been apart of the game.

Now, we just asked our fans to vote on an issue without providing them with the proper forum, and information to vote on the top players of the century. Here is what they said. You decide if it was fair?

Here are the selections by <u>NBC and MasterCard</u>:

NBC SELECTION / MASTER CARD SELECTION

IB-Lou Gehrig	IB-Lou Gehrig
Mark McGwire	Mark McGwire

<table>
<tr><td>

2B-Jackie Robinson
   Roger Hornby

3B-Mike Schmidt
   Brooks Robinson

SS-Cal Ripken, Jr.
Ernie Banks
Honus Wagner

C-Johnny Bench
   Yogi Berra

OF-Babe Ruth
   Hank Aaron
   Willie Mays
   Stan Musial
   Mickey Mantle
   Ted Williams
   Joe DiMaggio

</td><td>

2B-Jackie Robinson
   Roger Hornby

3B-Mike Schmidt
   Brooks Robinson

SS-Cal Ripken, Jr.
Ernie Banks

C-Johnny Bench
   Yogi Berra

OF-Babe Ruth
   Hank Aaron
   Ted Williams
   Willie Mays
   Joe DiMaggio
   Mickey Mantle
   Ty Cobb

</td></tr>
</table>

NBC'S	MASTER CARD'S
Ty Cobb	Ken Griffey, Jr.
Pete Rose	Pete Rose
Ken Griffey, Jr.	

<table>
<tr><td>

PIT-Nolan Ryan
   Sandy Koufax
   Bob Gibson
   Cy Young
   Walter Johnson
   Roger Clemens
   Warren Spahn
   Lefty Grove
   Christy Mathewson

</td><td>

PIT-Nolan Ryan
   Sandy Koufax
   Cy Young
   Roger Clemens
   Bob Gibson
   Walter Johnson

</td></tr>
</table>

Both teams left off two of the greatest outfielders of our time. The consummate lead off hitter in Rickey Henderson, and the consummate classic master hitter, in Tony Gwynn were no where to be found. One of top voting receivers in the HOF, Tom Seaver, also did not make it.

I think this is adequate proof that something really needs to be done immediately to clear up voting for the Hall of Fame.

//

HIDDEN MIND-SET

John Rocker is a relief pitcher for the Atlanta Braves at this writing. He has recently developed a habit of expressing apparently how he feels about people in the U.S.A. that are unlike him.

He has made racial insults to a lot of people from different ethical backgrounds. He started with the fans in New York, and ended with attacks on teammates.

John Rocker at this time is a confused and frustrated young man. He might change some time in the future, but right now he has problems. He has problems not related to a fastball, or a batter. However, he is only expressing the "hidden mind-set" already established in the country.

Part of Chapter VII deals with the mind-set of people such as John Rocker.

When I considered who would be considered for the top players of the 20th century, the main objective of my concern was for this to be a fair voting assessment.

The spirit of John Rocker still lives in baseball and the world. Sometimes this spirit is quiet and goes without a voice and a face…remaining as thoughts.

Rocker is not the only player still in baseball who feels the way he did when he expressed his opinion recently. He just put a face and personality on it.

Rocker's feelings have been publicly known. In case you were out of the country at the time, he had negative feelings about foreigners, gays, and people with AIDS, Asians, Native Americans, New Yorkers, New York Mets fans, and Blacks. He asked the question, how did these people get in this country? That's another book.

Here are examples of the mind-set displayed by the John Rockers of America:

(1) Hank Aaron brakes "Babe Ruth's so-called record. He establishes the real homerun record (755), but Babe Ruth is still considered the homerun champion.
(2) Josh Gibson establishes a so-called homerun record at 962. Ruth still gets the credit for his record. Gibson is not considered.
(3) Ruth hits 60 homeruns in a season. He's the accepted HR champion.
(4) Gibson hits 84 HRs in one year, and 74 HRs in another). Not acknowledged.
(5) Mark McGwire hits 70 homeruns, and is given credit for braking Ruth's record not Gibson's.

(6) McGwire, and Sosa, hit more than 60 HRs twice at this writing and Gibson hit more than 60 at least five times. Ruth does not lead in the most hits, RBI's, or HRs, but he is the player of the century. None of the other players except for Aaron are even close to being recognized for that honor.

(7) Josh Gibson was the only player in history to hit a ball out of the old Yankee Stadium. A feat not generally known in baseball. In the defense of John Rocker I will say this. He is young and spoke without thinking as do a lot of young people. Although this nation has not had a history of forgiveness, baseball has with certain people and not particularly of a racial nature.

The biggest enemy Rocker is going to face is himself. If his heart is in the right place, he probably will continue on to be what appears to be a promising career.

I heard the cries of the public to crucify him, and gave the Atlanta Braves and major league baseball management orders to trade or ostracize him.

What is the crying about? When we should have had protesting in baseball we didn't.

When Ruth played he was the baseball god to 98% of the status quo baseball world. There was no mind-set or desire to want to change from that regardless of how great a potential that person could be.

Jackie Robinson, Larry Doby, and definitely Hank Aaron experienced the pressures they did mostly because of that mind-set.

These were facts the fans should have been abreast of before voting on the players of the century. I am sure all fans would have been fair.

SPECIAL RECOGNITION FOR NL DEVELOPMENT

1.) <u>Thompson, Frank P.</u>
Active From 1885-   Position: Owner, Pioneer
Teams: Argyle Hotel Athletics, and the Cuban Giants

In 1886, Frank Thompson was a headwaiter at Long Island's Argyle Hotel. Frank recruited players for entertainment from the Philadelphia Keystones to work at the hotel, and he formed a baseball team...entertainment as it were.

After the tourist season, the team added more players to form the Cuban Giants, and toured as the first Black team. They were Colored champions in 1887, and 1888. They were considered the top club at that time.

Frank Thompson didn't plan to create the first Black professional baseball team, but because he did, the early African-Americans, and dark skin Hispanics had a place to go. It gave them "chance and opportunity."

The Cuban Giants were not just a Black professional team, they were the best. They only lasted until 1899.

Years after their duration, teams copied their style of play. They were THE team at the close of the Nineteenth century.

Because of the Cuban Giants, teams like the Chicago Unions, the Page Fence Giants, and the League of Colored Baseball Clubs (L.O.C.B.P.) were able to provide a format for Black and Hispanic players.

2.) <u>Craig, John (Homer)</u>
Active From: 1935-44   Position: <u>Umpire</u>
League: NNL

One of the better umpires of the NNL. He spent 12 years at the top in Black baseball.

3.) <u>Gholston, Bert E.</u>
Active From: 1923-43   Position: <u>Umpire</u>
Leagues: NNL, EWL

One of the very best umpires in the NL. He arbitrated for 22 years in the NNL, and one year in the EWL, its only year.

4.) <u>League Of Colored Baseball Clubs</u>
Active From: 1887 (One week)

Special recognition should be given to the League of Colored Baseball Clubs for their attempt to bridge the gap, and offer an avenue to Black and Hispanic players of professional quality.

Even though the league did not last but a week, it was long enough to plant ideas in the minds of future owners, and pioneers of Black baseball…like Sol White, and Rube Foster.

The following is a list of those teams:

    1.) Baltimore Lord Baltimores
    2.) Boston Resolutes
    3.) Cincinnati Browns
    4.) Louisville Falls Citys
    5.) New York Gorhams
    6.) Philadelphia Pythians
    7.) Pittsburgh Keystones
    8.) Washington Capital Citys

5.) <u>The Argyle Hotel Athletics</u>
Active: 1885

This was the team that gave rise to the first professional Black team…the Cuban Giants. With players from the Philadelphia Keystones, an amateur team whose players worked as waiters at the Argyle Hotel in Babylon, New York. They played for the summer tourist.

Because of the their success, John Lang, a White entrepreneur managed them until selling them to Walter Cook in 1886. At this point, they became the Cuban Giants; the first professional Black teams. The Cuban Giants' duration was from 1885 to 1899. This was over 100 years ago, and they were considered the best team of their era. They were the top attraction, and other teams imitated them.

6. <u>Moses Fleetwood Walker</u>
Active: From 1884-   Position: <u>OF</u>

Moses was the first African-American professional major league baseball player—before Jackie Robinson. In 1884, he played with the Toledo team of the American Association, which was on a par with the National and American Leagues of today and quality at that time. This was before the American League was formed in 1901.

Fleetwood played in 42 games as a catcher and batted .263. His brother Welday, a second baseman who had to convert to the outfield because of harassment, later joined him. Welday only played 5 games and hit .222.

According to the Toledo Blade, in a game with Louisville, Moses was "hissed and insulted." He later experienced the same thing with Newark in 1887 as part of a battery with George Stovey. In July of 1887, Cap Anson (HOF) 1st baseman, and manager of the Chicago White Stockings had a scheduled game with Newark. He vowed not to let his team play if Stovey, and Walker played, thus the "color line" was established in 1887.

CATEGORY SUMMARIES FOR THE HOF

Category I

Bankhead, Samuel Howard, SS, CF, 2B, LF
Beckwith, John, SS, 3B, C
Brewer, Chester Arthur, P
Dixon, Herbert (Rap), RF
Donaldson, John Wesley, P
Hill, J. Preston, (Pete), CF, LF
Jenkins, Clarence (Fats), OF
Johnson, Grant (Homerun), SS
Lundy, Richard (Dick, King Richard), SS
Mackey, Raleigh (Biz), C
Mendez, Jose' (Joe, The Black Diamond), P
Monroe, William (Bill), 2B, 3B, SS
Oms, Alejandro (El Caballero, Walla Walla), CF
<u>Petway, Bruce (Buddy), C</u>
<u>Poles, Spottswood (Spot), CF</u>
Radcliffe, Theodore Roosevelt (Double Duty) C, P
Redding, Richard (Cannonball, Dick), P
***Rogan Wilbur (Joe, Bullet), P, OF, 2B**
Santop, Louis (Top, Big Bertha), C
Smith, Hilton (Lee), P
***Stearns, Norman Thomas (Turkey), CF**
Suttles, George (Mule), IB, LF
Taylor, Benjamin H. (Ben), IB
Thomas, Clinton Cyrus (Clint, Hawk), CF
<u>Torriente, Cristobal (Carlos), CF</u>
***Williams, Joseph (Smokey Joe, Cyclone, Yank), P**
Wilson, Ernest Judson (Jud, Boojum), 3B, IB

CATEGORY II

Boyd, Robert, Richard (Bob, The Rope), IB
***Doby, Lawrence Eugene (Larry L. D.), 2B, 3B**
Howard, Elston (Gene, Ellie), C
Minoso, Saturnino, Orestes, Arrieta, Armas (Minnie), 3B
Newcombe, Donald (Don, Newk), P

CATEGORY III

Allen, Newton (Newt), 2b, SS, 3B, OF
Barnhill, Dave (Skinny), P
Easter, Luscious (Luke), OF, IB
Fowler, John W. (Bud), 2B, 3B, P
Grant, Ulysses F. (Frank), 2B
Jones, Stuart (Slim), P
Smith, Charles (Chino, Charlie), OF
Stovey, George Washington, P.

CATEGORY IV

Bolden, Edward (Ed Chief), Owner, Officer
Greenlee, William Augustus (Gus, Big Red), Owner
Leland, Frank C. -Manager, Owner
Manley, Effa—Owner, Officer
McMahan, Jesse Rod (Jess), Owner, Officer
O'Neill, John Jordon (Buck, Foots, Nancy), Manager
Posey, Cumberland Willis, Jr. (Cum) Officer, Owner
Taylor, Charles Isham (C. I.) Manager, Officer
Thompson, Frank P.—Owner, Founder
Wilkinson, James Leslie—Owner, Officer, Inventor
White, Solomon (Sol), Coach, Manager, Officer

* Indicates recent HOF inductee.

<u>BOOK SUMMARY-HOPE UNBORN</u>

My hope is that this book has been educational, particularly to our youth. My belief is that it will be information giving, and solution oriented. My dream is that the struggle against racism will be helped, and hopefully it will help ease the pain of omission, and help bond our history and culture so that it will be realized anew.

The realization is that history cannot be done over on this matter, but an attempt can be made to make it right. Recognition and acceptance by the total community of baseball in America will go along ways to satisfy that correction. The total community of baseball has been in denial about the real truth since the mid-1880's. Other sports have had similar problems, but baseball is basically the area of our concern in this book.

From the time the "color line" was drawn in the 1880's, American professional baseball has had a piece of their puzzle missing. Human rights were violated because everyone was not allowed to participate at their own will. The total major league package was denied.

Today, the "color line" is dropped on the playing field, but a line still exist in almost all areas of American professional sports. It exists in management, coaching (managing), administrative offices, ownership, marketing, and even the media. Imagine if the Black players from the Negro Leagues would have been marketed like the status quo players. Little kids (if informative, White kids as well) buying Josh Gibson's or Satchel Paige's products, or following their ledger around the country.

Ask the Black and minority coaches who have been denied "chance and opportunity" in baseball, football, and basketball about the problem? If they are old enough to be coaches/managers, then they are old enough to have been racially denied.

I have no desire to show where status quo players who deserve to be in the Hall of Fame shouldn't be. That would defeat the fact that there are deserving Negro League players who should be in there. The difference is that even though the leagues were separated physically, they were still equal in a lot of ways. Today, every time a Black/Hispanic player competes they reinforce that.

What was not equal was the fact that they couldn't play together, laugh together, fraternize together, cry together, or share life as big league ball players and human beings together. Who knows, some could have really been the best of friends, and other relationships could have grown pretty much like today's players with the conditions of time being the only difference.

Recently, the baseball community (Feb. '99) begin to honor Hank Aaron, as he should have been long before now, and just as status quo players of similar stature and celebrity have been. While I appreciate the forward movement baseball has taken, there always appear to be reminders of the past taking on disguises of honesty, truth, and decency.

The next day after the Aaron honor and celebration, an article proclaimed in the Atlanta Journal-Constitution, <u>"Aaron Key Issue This Night."</u> After some discussion about the festivities of the evening, including the presence of President Clinton, the writer decided to state— "This may offend some, but this was a time for honoring a man, not expounding on history which should have been lived down by now. To dwell on the progress made, not the ills of the past, the beautiful world that has been set out there for both black and white to thrive together.

Not to drag every skeleton out of the closet from Rosa Parks to Rodney King, whose names came across the podium."

He continued, "I'm reminded of the beer commercial in which the lead voice says, 'Let it alone, Louie. Drop it, Louie.' Drop it and let's move forward, not backward."

Rosa Parks has now become a skeleton in the closet for the American household, according to this writer of the article. I don't think that's true for most African-Americans, and Hank Aaron is an African-American, and part of his past was "ills of the past".

The problem with dropping it and moving on is that it gets swept under the rug.

The crux of the problem is that since the beginning of the "color line," Blacks and Whites did not thrive together. The "color line" was a form of sweeping it under the proverbial rug. When Hank Aaron started playing in the major leagues in 1954, sixty years after the "color line," Blacks and Whites did not thrive together.

Later, in the 60's when Rosa Parks made her mark in history, and even more recently for Rodney King. I promise you, that those walks through history were not signs that Blacks and Whites thrived together even today.

I am proud for Henry Aaron, the Black community, and the entire community of baseball for this long over-due recognition to Aaron, but one honor's night does not a panacea make. I don't know who spoke at the celebration, but the fact that it's a point of reference means that there is still work to be done in the areas of sensitivity, recognition, and acceptance. After all, that is what this book is about. The writer of this article cannot set the tone for feelings, societal issues, and progress. This has been the problem from the beginning.

If you want to set the tone for progress, and societal issues, we can start by giving recognition to the Negro League baseball players who had to thrive alone and still have not received their overdue reward. Many of which served in World Wars I & II. You would have thought that the Jackie Robinson and Satchel Paige stories would have taught them something. Every time we learn what history has taught us, we drag skeletons out of the closet. A skeleton coming out of the closet is apparently upsetting to some of us, probably because we have something we are not able or willing to deal with, but that's not the skeleton's problem.

Leaving it alone will not make us "move forward." Having a problem which we do have, and not dealing with it, doesn't make it go away. It will resurface somewhere else. Like calling Mark McGwire the new "homerun king," instead of recognizing him as the seasonal modern day homerun champion. I saw this on a poster recently.

Enter talk about the power of words and labels.

We can all agree that Aaron deserves this honor, but all I heard during the 1998 season was how Mark McGwire, or Sammy Sosa would be the new homerun champion. Then toward the end of the season, all we heard was about McGwire becoming the new homerun king. I don't think this problem has been solved. If there is one writer who thinks this way, there are many more (as indicated by the Hall of Fame voting). No wonder we have a problem making things the way it should be.

The all-time greatest professional baseball players are often stated to be Babe Ruth, Ty Cobb, Joe DiMaggio, or even Lou Gehrig. I contend that the greatest all-time players (Black or White) could not have come from a time during the "color line," because all of the best players did not get a chance to play <u>together</u>. At least, they did not get a chance to prove that they were the greatest.

The same truth that says, "Columbus discovered America," and not who really did, is the same truth that says Babe Ruth held the record (60) for the most homeruns in a season. What season was that, and did you see any Black faces on the field? or Josh Gibson held the records (84 & 74), and did you see any White faces on the field? I think not, nevertheless, Ruth was given that credit until 1998 not Gibson…Why?

There are similar records from the status quo league establishing that league as THE only major league with major records accepted. (See chapter VII)

Because baseball has been set up as the All-American sport, it supposedly represents everything good and right with America. Since we all want to feel good about America, lets correct the wrong in baseball, and maybe it will influence other avenues of our country.

I was recently watching a collectible show, and a woman had a baseball signed by Saduhara Oh.

Mr. Oh is the all-time homerun champion in Japan with over 800 homeruns. Oh was given credit by the baseball owner, and the appraiser as having been the first player to brake Babe Ruth's homerun record.

What does this mean? It means no regard for Josh Gibson, and no respect for Hank Aaron who is the only true champion of the four men.

Why are records from Japan ready to be accepted before records that are made in our own country? Did the appraiser know that the stadiums in Japan are much smaller than the stadiums in America?

If the Negro Major League records are accepted along with the NL players into the HOF, then it is reasonable to assume that all NML records recoverable from 1920 to 1952 should be accepted.

Why is that time the most important time? Even though the Negro Leagues go back into the 19th century, they were officially organized in 1920. When Jackie Robinson made his debut in 1947, and even three or four years later the majority of the best Negro League players were still in the Negro Leagues.

The demise of talent was really felt in the mid fifties with the lost of players like Ernie Banks, Hank Aaron, Willie Mays, Monte Irvin, Junior Gilliam, Don Newcombe, Elston Howard, Minnie Minoso, and others.

It doesn't appear to be a problem today accepting records of the status quo players of the past. Status quo players of the past and their records are often mentioned during broadcasts, sports shows, interviews, or memorabilia comparisons.

However, the great NL players are rarely mentioned, and particularly their records.

The so-called baseball experts have not been challenged to know and use the facts on Josh Gibson, Buck Leonard, etc. like they have repeatedly done with Babe Ruth, Lou Gehrig, and other status quo stars of that era.

Finally, someone should speak out for equal rights of the Negro Leagues. Someone should get the records straighten out about what really happen in Black and White baseball in America.

If it embarrasses certain people because of what happened in the past, think of how long it has not been dealt with, and what problems it has caused those people who have been neglected their places in baseball history. Someone needs to educate our youths on this dark past of American history, and get the message out. I am someone, and I am getting it out. SELAH!

<u>ABBREVIATIONS</u>

1.) ACC—Atlantic Coast Conference
2.) ACT—American College Test
3.) B-Game—An additional game played during spring training to allow management to let players get in the right amount of playing time, and extra time for players to be evaluated.
4.) B. A.—Batting Average
5.) E.C.L.—Eastern Colored League
6.) E. R. A.—Earned Run Average—Runs given up by a pitcher, not including runs made because of errors.
7.) E. W. L.—East-West League
8.) G. P. A.—Grade Point Average
9.) HOF—Hall of Fame
10.) L. O. C. B. C.—League of Colored Baseball Clubs (1887)
11.) N. A. L.—Negro American League
12.) N L—Negro League(s)
13.) N. M. L.—Negro Major League(s); NNL, ECL, NAL
14.) N N L—Negro National League
15.) M L—major league
16.) U. S. B. L.—United Stated Baseball League
17.) BBWAA—Baseball Writers Association of America

<u>ALL REFERENCE MATERIALS</u>

<u>FILMS—That contributed to the source of information in this book.</u>

(1) Kings of the Hill (Baseball's Forgotten Men)
By San Pedro Productions, LTD
Executive Producer, Tom Roy
Producers, Rob Ruck, & Molly Youngling

(2) Baseball
Corporation for Public Broadcasting
A Florentine Films Production

(3) Ken "The Kid" Burns
Lynn "The Babe" Novick
**<u>Written by Geoffrey C. "The Mahatma" Ward & Ken "The Kid"
Burns</u>**

(4) The Court-martial of Jackie Robinson
<u>Turner Pictures, Inc.</u>
<u>Executive Producers-Frank von Zerneck & Robert M. Sertner</u>
**<u>Actors—Andre` Braugher, Ruby Dee, Don Hood, Howard French,
Jim Beaver, and Travis Sword</u>**

Main Narrators
Mario Cuomo—Ex Governor of New York
Shelby Foote—Writer
Riley Stewart—Chicago American Giants
Sammy Haynes—K. C. Monarchs
Buck O'Neil—K. C. Monarchs
Bob Costas—Broadcaster
Ozzie Davis—Actor
Harold Tinker—Pittsburgh Crawfords
Monte Irvin—Newark Eagles, New York Giants
Satchel Paige—Many NL teams, Cleveland Indians, St. Louis Browns
Teenie Harris—Pittsburgh Crawfords
Mal Godde—Journalist
Wendell Smith—Writer
John Holway—Historian
Judge Norris Coleman—Historian
Bob Thurman—Homestead Grays

Buck Leonard—Homestead Grays
Charles "Chub" Feeney—New York Giant Executive
Connie Johnson—K. C. Monarchs
Double Duty Radcliffe—Negro League player
Billy Herman—Chicago Cubs
Curt Flood—St Louis Cardinals
Ted Williams—Boston Red Sox
Birdie Tebbetts, Manager of the Cincinnati Reds.
Vin Scully—Broadcaster (For my Dodger Blues)
Red Barber—Broadcaster (For my Dodger Blues)
John Thorn—Historian
George Plimpton—Writer
Daniel Okrent—Editor

NEWSPAPERS & MAGAZINES—Used in the book as a source of information.

1995 NCAA Division I Graduation Rates Report
Amsterdam News
Atlanta Journal-Constitution
Associated Press
Chicago Defender
Pittsburgh Courier
Toledo Blade
Sports Illustrated—Online
"This Day in Sports"
1995 TK Publishers
TOPPS Magazine (1992 summer issue #11)
USA Today
The Sporting News
Sports Cards (magazine) July 1992
Publisher & Editor Allan Kaye

REFERENCE BOOKS-That were used as a source of reference in this book.

1) The Biographical Encyclopedia of the Negro Leagues
    By James A. Riley
    Published by Carroll & Graf Pub. Inc. New York, 1994

2) When the Game Was Black & White
    By Bruce Chadwick
    Published by Abbeville Press N. Y. 1992

3) Negro Leagues
    The Story of Black Baseball
    By Jacob Margolies
    Published by Frank Watts 1993

4) The Invisible Men
    Life in Baseball's Negro Leagues
    By Donn Rogogin
    Published by Atheneun Publisher

<u>PEOPLE OF CONTRIBUTION</u>—People who contributed to the source of this book.

Rubye A. Carswell (wife) information, technical
Elmer Knox (Negro League player)
Jimmy "Squab" Hill (Negro League player)
Richard Lapchick (Sports authority)
Branch Rickey (signed Jackie Robinson)
Gilbert Jenkins, Jr. (father-in-law) information
James Weldon Johnson (words from song)
John B. Holway (writer)
Jerry Smart (contributor)
Joseph Tucker (technical contributor)
John Watkins (Negro League player)
Melzie Pressley (information)
Eugene Starks (informatiom)
Gertrude Jenkins (mother-in-law) information
Cesar Capers (technical contributor)
Doug Garr (Sports authority)
Furman Bisher (writer)
George (Marty) Martin Carswell (contributor)
Reo (Refrom) Nicole Carswell (contributor
Phil Pepe (writer-Sports authority)
Marion Wilson (writer)
Wanda Jones (contributor)
Cecil S. Clark (Information)

ABOUT THE AUTHOR

I was born in the early forties in Lakeland, Florida. It was a time at the ending of World War II. It was a time to put the country back together, and we did in some ways. As an African-American, my goals were limited, but my parents and grandparents were proponents of education. So, off to college it was for me after stardom in the Florida State Negro League Baseball Tournament. I wanted to play professionally and had a chance, but I was overruled by my parents/grandparents.

My choice of course would more than likely be a Black Historical College or University (HBCU). Since my grandfather was a Baptist minister and a trustee at Florida Memorial College, an HBCU, and a friend of the college president, I would say that in those years my choice was already made.

For thirty-seven years I worked professional as a teacher, social worker, youth counselor, coach, and educator. Voluntarily, I have worked as a college and prep school recruiter, group leader, and recreation supervisor.

Educationally, I have a B. S. degree in Education with special graduate training in counseling. The schools I have attended are Florida Memorial College, Trenton State Teacher's College, and Rider University.

Some of my most enjoyable memories have been when I have helped students to achieve their goal of reaching college or prep school on a scholarship.

I have been married for thirty-seven years to a wonderful wife, Ruybe and we have two children, Martin and Reo. Currently, I am retired and living in metro Atlanta, Georgia.